HEGEL

AMS PRESS
NEW YORK

HEGEL

BY

EDWARD CAIRD, LL.D.

PROFESSOR OF MORAL PHILOSOPHY,
UNIVERSITY OF GLASGOW

WILLIAM BLACKWOOD AND SONS
EDINBURGH AND LONDON
1883

Library of Congress Cataloging in Publication Data

Caird, Edward, 1835-1908.
   Hegel.

   Original ed. issued as v. 7 of Philosophical classics
for English readers.
   1. Hegel, Georg Wilhelm Friedrich, 1770-1831.
I. Series: Philosophical classics for English readers.
B2947.C3 1972   193   71-181924
ISBN 0-404-01362-7

Reprinted from the edition of 1883, Edinburgh and London
First AMS edition published in 1972
Manufactured in the United States of America

AMS PRESS INC.
NEW YORK, N. Y.   10003

PREFATORY NOTE.

THE main authorities for the life of Hegel are the biographies of Rosenkranz and Haym,—the former a pupil and devoted disciple of Hegel, the latter a critic whose opposition to Hegel's philosophical principles has passed into a kind of personal bitterness, which misconstrues his simplest actions. Some additional details may be derived from Hotho ('Vorstudien für Leben und Kunst'), from Ruge ('Aus früherer Zeit'), and from Klaiber ('Hölderlin, Hegel, und Schelling'). The books and articles written in Germany for or against the Hegelian philosophy it is impossible to enumerate, for almost every one who has written about philosophy in recent times has written about Hegel. Daub, Marheineke, Göschel, Rosenkranz, Erdmann, Gabler, Vatke, and Ruge are the names of only a few of the most important adherents of the school. The ablest attack upon Hegelianism which I have seen is by Dr A. Schmid ('Entwickelungsgeschichte der Hegelischen

Logik'). To English readers Hegel was first introduced in the powerful statement of his principles by Dr Hutchison Stirling. Mr Wallace, in the introduction to his translation of the lesser Logic, and Mr Harris, the editor of the American 'Speculative Journal,' have since done much to illustrate various aspects of the Hegelian philosophy. Other English writers, such as the late Professor Green, Mr Bradley, Professor Watson, and Professor Adamson, who have not directly treated of Hegel, have been greatly influenced by him. Mr Seth has recently written an interesting account of the movement from Kant to Hegel.

CONTENTS.

CHAP.		PAGE
I.	LEHRJAHRE — THE SCHOOL AND THE UNIVERSITY,	1
II.	WANDERJAHRE—HEGEL AS A PRIVATE TUTOR AT BERNE AND FRANKFORT — HIS PHILOSOPHY IN ITS DEVELOPMENT,	13
III.	HEGEL AND SCHELLING—JENA, 1800-1807,	45
IV.	HEGEL AFTER THE BATTLE OF JENA — THE SCHOOL AT NÜRNBERG,	65
V.	HEGEL AS A PROFESSOR AT HEIDELBERG AND BERLIN— HIS CHARACTER AND INFLUENCE,	77
VI.	THE PROBLEM OF PHILOSOPHY—STATEMENT OF IT BY KANT, FICHTE, SCHELLING, AND HEGEL,	112
VII.	THE PRINCIPLE OF CONTRADICTION AND THE IDEA OF SPIRIT,	134

VIII. THE HEGELIAN LOGIC, . . . 151

IX. THE APPLICATION OR DEVELOPMENT OF THE LOGICAL IDEA—RELATION OF THE HEGELIAN PRINCIPLE TO CHRISTIANITY—THE HEGELIAN PHILOSOPHY AFTER HEGEL, . 186

HEGEL.

CHAPTER I.

LEHRJAHRE—THE SCHOOL AND THE UNIVERSITY.

THE great movement of thought which characterises the nineteenth century is a movement through negation to reaffirmation, through destruction to reconstruction,—in Carlyle's language, through the "everlasting no" to the "everlasting yea." Its great men are men who, like Mirabeau, have "swallowed all formulas," yet have not in the process lost their faith in the spiritual powers and destiny of man; whose emancipation from the weight of the past, from the life of custom and tradition, has only revealed to them more clearly the permanent basis of human faith and hope, the eternal rock on which all human beliefs and institutions are built. Their greatness is measured by the completeness with which the whole movement of the time, negative and positive, has mirrored itself in their intellectual history, and by the degree in which they have mastered its striving elements, and brought them to a unity as factors of their own inner life. Their weakness is measured by the degree in which they have become the passive organs and spokesmen of one or other of the opposite principles of revolt or reaction, or have yielded successively to the alternate tides of popular feeling as they swayed from one extreme to the other. No man, indeed, who is in the midst of such a social and intellectual movement, and not yet looking upon it from the vantage-ground of history, can completely gather into himself the whole spirit of an age, or enter with the sympathy of complete understanding into both of its opposed enthusiasms. No man, even if he does so, can be so far independent of the process in which he is a part, as never in the hour of revolt to confuse anarchy with liberty, and never, when the time of reconstruction comes, to be tempted to use for the new building some of the "wood, hay, or stubble" of the old which has been tried in the fire and found wanting. No man is allowed to play providence or to escape paying the penalty of the limitations of his individuality and his time. Any approximation, however, to such a comprehensive result,—any life that escapes the fanaticism of abstract denial or abstract reaffirmation of the ideals and faiths of the past, and escapes it not merely by applying the leaden rule of temporary expediency and ordinary common-sense, but by the way of a deeper insight, and a firmer grasp of the unity that binds together all the aspects of the many-sided reality,—any life, in short, which does not merely change with the changing time, but has a true progress or development in it, must be of the highest interest and instruction for us. In it, as in a kind of microcosm, we can spell out more clearly the lesson which in the wider macrocosm it is so hard to read. It is this comprehensiveness of experience, this openness to both of the leading currents of tendency in their time, and this constant effort—more or less successful and on a wider or smaller scale—to reach a point of view from which these tendencies might be understood and harmonised, that gives such value to the life and writings of men so different in every other respect as Wordsworth and Carlyle, as Comte and Goethe. It is this also which lends interest to the great movement of German philosophy which began with Kant, and the ultimate meaning of which was expressed by Hegel. For that movement was, above all, an attempt to find a way *through* the modern principles of subjective freedom—the very principle which produced the Reformation of the sixteenth and the Revolution of the eighteenth century—to a reconstruction of the intellectual and moral order on which man's life had been based in the past.

George William Frederic Hegel was born at Stuttgart, the capital of Würtemberg, on the 27th August 1770, five years before the birth of Schelling, eleven years after the birth of Schiller, both of whom, like himself, were Würtembergers. The inhabitants of the Swabian highlands have long been distinguished from the other Germans by peculiarities of dialect and character, by a mixture of shrewdness and simplicity, of religious enthusiasm and speculative free-thinking, which has led Mr Seeley to name them the Scots of Germany. By position and race, Swabia belongs to the South, by religion to the North, a circumstance which of itself tended to keep alive an intenser religious and intellectual life in a country that might regard itself as a kind of outpost or advanced-guard of Protestantism. In their general characteristics the Swabians form a sort of middle term between the different branches of the German nation. The hard rationalism and practical energy which distinguishes the Protestant North, and especially Prussia, is in them softened and widened by what the Germans call the *Gemüthlichkeit* of a southern race, and has given rise to a certain meditative depth of nature, which sometimes leads to abstruseness and mysticism, but is less apt to let its consciousness of the wholeness or organic unity of truth be broken and disturbed by the antagonisms of reflection. It is worth noting in this reference, that while the first two leaders in the great philosophical movement of Germany, Kant and Fichte—those who especially asserted the freedom and independence of man, and set the self above the not-self—belonged to the North; the last two, Schelling and Hegel, those who rose above this one-sided idealism to a consciousness of the spirituality of the world and of man's unity with it and with his fellow-men, belonged to the South, and indeed to this same region of Swabia.

Hegel was of a family which traced its descent to one Johann Hegel, who was driven from Carinthia by the Austrian persecution of the Protestants towards the end of the sixteenth century, and which, during the seventeenth and eighteenth centuries, gave many of its sons to the humbler branches of the civil service of Würtemberg. His father, of whom we know little, was an officer in the fiscal service, a man of the orderly habits and the conservative instincts natural to his place. His mother, whom he lost in his thirteenth year, and of whom he always cherished a grateful remembrance, seems to have been a woman of considerable education and intelligence. He had a younger brother, Louis, who became a soldier—and a sister, Christiane, between whom and the philosopher there appears to have been a strong bond of affection. We catch a glimpse of a quiet *bourgeois* household, governed by a spirit of honesty, economy, and industry, and in which the education of the children was the most important concern. After receiving some instruction from his mother, Hegel was sent to a so-called Latin school in his fifth year, and in his seventh to the gymnasium of his native city. He seems to have been distinguished only as a thoroughly teachable boy, ready to acquire knowledge of any kind, but with no predominant taste or capacity in any one direction. He showed from the first the patient methodical habits of the race of civil servants from which he had sprung, and was, in short, that uninteresting character, "the good boy who takes prizes in every class, including the prize for good conduct." At the age of fourteen he began to keep a diary—it was the age of diaries—but this did not indicate in him any premature tendency to self-consciousness or self-analysis. In fact he found nothing particular to chronicle in it, except the progress of his reading, and sometimes he uses it merely as a means for practising himself in the writing of Latin. There is perhaps a tinge of boyish pedantry in the premature seriousness with which he records the progress of his studies. A strong expression of affection and gratitude to one of his teachers, called Löffler, who had given him private instruction in addition to the regular class lessons, and who died when Hegel was in his fifteenth year, is almost the only utterance of individual feeling to be found in the diary,—"How often and how happily did he sit by me, and I by him, in the little chamber!" For the rest, the contents of the diary are an echo of the enlightened views of the day, which Hegel heard from his teachers, and read in the popular text-books of science and philosophy which they put into his hands. In this spirit he points out the evils of intolerance, and the necessity of thinking for one's self, condemns the superstitions of the vulgar, notices the similarity of the miracles of all ages and nations, and suggests that there is not much difference between the purchase of heaven's favour by direct offerings to the gods and the modern substitute of gifts to the Church,—all with the wisdom of a little Solon of the *Aufklärung*.

The one study, however, which seems to have taken a deep hold upon him, and which towards the end of his school years awakened him for the first time to some freshness and originality of remark, was the study of Greek poetry. The tragedies of Sophocles especially cast an abiding charm on him; and the "Antigone," which he always considered the masterpiece of dramatic poetry, was twice translated by him—once in prose, and again, at the university, in verse. The elective affinity which thus drew Hegel to the pure undefiled well of Greek art lay very deep in his nature, and produced the greatest effect in all his subsequent work, both positively and negatively. Even during his youth he seems scarcely to have felt any charm in the romance of diseased sentimentalism for which Werther set the fashion in Germany, and which was afterwards repeated in weaker echoes by Schlegel and others. Nor, though as we shall see he afterwards came under the power of Christian and romantic art, did he ever feel anything but repulsion for that formless emotional tendency which was often in his day confused with it. "Early penetrated by the nobility and beauty of Greece," says Rosenkranz, "he never could recognise genuine Christianity in a form which excludes the earnest serenity of antique art." His usual universality of intelligent sympathy seemed to give way to a certain bitterness of antagonism when he was brought face to face with any example of the Rousseauist disease of self-consciousness; and even in a mystic like Hamann, who attracted him by the humorous riches of his thoughts, Hegel discovered an element of "hypochondria" to which he was unable entirely to reconcile himself. But Greek art came to him as the vision of a realised harmony of existence, in which there was no war of subject and object, of ideal and real; and even from his first contact with it, he found in it his native element. "At the name of Greece," as he declared to his students long afterwards, "the cultivated German feels himself at home. Europeans have their religion—what is transcendent and distant—from a further source, from the East, and especially from Syria; but what is here, what is present, science and art—all that makes life satisfying, and elevates and adorns it—we derive, directly or indirectly, from Greece."

Another important habit Hegel took with him from school. In his sixteenth year he had commenced the practice of making copious extracts from every book that interested him; and to judge from the manuscripts which are still preserved, he already found interest in almost every branch of science accessible to him. This habit he continued through life; so that there are very few important literary or scientific products of his time—indeed few great literary or scientific products of any time—of which he had not made a full analysis, and even copied out the principal parts. In this way he gradually accumulated a considerable number of well-arranged commonplace-books—for in everything he was exact and orderly—and, what was still more valuable, he acquired the habit not only of grasping the general meaning of the authors he read, but of entering into their specific quality, and appreciating even that subtle flavour of individuality which is conveyed in the minute turns of style and phraseology. True culture, as he afterwards taught, must begin with a resolute self-effacement, with a purely receptive attitude; and it is only through such an attitude that we can attain to that vital criticism which is virtually the criticism of the object by itself. Speaking of the Pythagorean method of education, in which the pupil was condemned to silence for five years, Hegel says that, "in a sense, this duty of silence is the essential condition of all culture and learning. We must begin with being able to apprehend the thoughts of others, and this implies a disregarding of our own ideas. It is often said that the mind is to be cultured from the first by questions, objections, and answers, &c. In fact, such a method does not give to it real culture, but rather makes it external and superficial. By silence, by keeping ourselves to ourselves, we are not made poorer in spirit. Rather by it we gain the capacity of apprehending things as they really are, and the consciousness that subjective opinions and objections are good for nothing, so that we cease at last even to have them." This counsel is no doubt somewhat hard to follow, and it is not without danger of being misinterpreted in the case of minds whose vital power of reaction on what they have received is comparatively feeble. But for minds whose springs cannot be broken by any weight of information, who possess that "robust intellectual digestion which is equal to whole libraries," it is nothing less than intellectual salvation. At any rate it is certain that Hegel had proved it upon himself from the earliest years.

At the age of eighteen Hegel left the gymnasium for the university. Destined by his parents for the Church, he was sent with a bursary to the theological seminary of Tübingen—an institution in which some show of monastic discipline was kept up. The members of the "Stift" wore a peculiar dress, and were subjected to a somewhat petty system of punishments—generally by deprivation of the customary portion of wine at dinner—for all offences against the regular order of the place. Of course theology took the first place in the prescribed order of study, though the course was divided into a philosophical and a theological portion, the former occupying two, and the latter three years. There was at the time no one among the professors of Tübingen who was capable of permanently influencing and guiding a pupil like Hegel. Some of them acknowledged the influence of Kant, then the rising star of philosophy, so far as to make him an occasional subject of lecture, and even to pervert his principles to the support of the old system of doctrine—not a difficult thing with an author in whom the letter so often falls short of the spirit. But there was not among them even one thoroughly trained disciple of Kant, who could teach the new ideas with sympathy and intelligence. Accordingly Hegel soon learnt to take the university work as a routine to be got over with the minimum of attention, and we even find that he was specially reprimanded for the frequency with which he had incurred the penalties for absence from lecture. There is evidence, however, that he steadily pursued his reading in classical authors, adding to them many modern writers, especially Rousseau, whose works were the key to the great political movement then rapidly coming to a head in France. For such reading Hegel was well prepared by his previous training; for Rousseau transcended the individualistic commonplaces of the philosophical text-books, which Hegel had been patiently copying out at school, mainly in this, that his passionate fervour of belief, his native sympathy with the poorer classes, and his sense of social injustice, changed them from the light playthings of literature into the winged shafts of speech that make men mad. Hegel and his companions, among whom was Schelling—younger in years than Hegel, but much more precocious in intellectual development—formed a political club, in which the ideas of the Revolution were discussed; and Hegel, we are told, was distinguished among its members as the enthusiastic champion of liberty and fraternity. There was even a tradition—which has now been proved to refer to another time—that he and Schelling went out one fine spring morning to plant a tree of Liberty in the market-place of Tübingen. At any rate, it is certain that Hegel fully shared in the wonderful hopes which at the time stirred all that was generous and imaginative in Europe.

> "Bliss was it in that dawn to be alive,
> But to be young was very heaven."

For the rest, Hegel took part in all the usual incidents of German student life—its *camaraderie*, its conviviality, its enthusiastic friendships, and even, it would seem, its love-making, though with a certain staidness and sobriety which got him the nickname of "old man" or "old fellow." He was, we gather, genial and good-humoured in manner, and was generally liked by his fellow-students, but not thought to have any very great abilities. Yet he formed special ties of friendship with the two of his fellows in the Stift who afterwards showed original powers,—with Schelling, and with a young poet called Hölderlin, whose verses are filled with a kind of romantic longing for Hellenic art and poetry, similar to that which was more powerfully expressed by Schiller in his "Gods of Greece." Hegel's association with Hölderlin, with whom he is recorded to have studied Plato and Sophocles, was especially fitted to deepen in his mind the impressions which he already had received in the gymnasium from the literature of Greece. Towards the end of his university career, however, his attention began to be turned more definitely towards philosophy, especially in its relation to theology, and in connection therewith to the ethical works of Kant. And the few pages from his note-books which are quoted by Rosenkranz show already his characteristic power of concentrating his meaning in pithy sayings,—words winged at once with imagination and reflection, which strike their mark like a cannon-ball. He had indeed, as we shall see, already entered upon that course of modification and transformation of Kantian principles, out of which his own philosophy was to spring. These studies were, however, altogether hidden from the authorities of the Stift, who, when he left Tübingen in 1793, dismissed him with a certificate that he was a man of good parts and character, somewhat fitful in his work, with little gift of speech; and that he was fairly well acquainted with theology and philology, but had bestowed no attention whatever on philosophy.

CHAPTER II.

WANDERJAHRE.—HEGEL AS A PRIVATE TUTOR AT BERNE AND FRANKFORT.—HIS PHILOSOPHY IN ITS DEVELOPMENT.

THERE is very little to record of Hegel's outward life in the six years after he left the university. The first three were spent by him in the Swiss city of Berne, as tutor in an aristocratic family of the name of Von Tschugg; and the last three in a similar position in the house of a Frankfort merchant called Gogel. Of the special relations between Hegel and his employers or pupils we hear nothing; nor is anything of importance recorded of his various friends and acquaintances in Switzerland, though his biographer has printed the journal of an excursion which he made with two of them in the Bernese Oberland. A few letters from his friends Hölderlin and Schelling kept him aware of the progress of the philosophical movement in Germany, and it was probably in order to get nearer the literary centre that in 1796 he applied to Hölderlin to help him to a situation in Frankfort. In one of his letters to Schelling he expresses an amused weariness of the petty plots and family cabals that made up the politics of the little aristocratic canton of Berne; and, no doubt, his strong political interest also made him desire to be in a better position for observing the great events which were then changing the face of Germany and Europe. In Frankfort, besides, he had the society of his old friend Hölderlin, and through him he was brought into close relations with another friend — a forgotten poet and philosopher called Sinclair—whose influence helped to draw him to the study of the Christian mystics, as well as of the romantic art and poetry of the middle ages.

As regards the development of Hegel's philosophy, however, these six uneventful years were the most important period of his life. It was his period of fermentation, in which the many elements of culture he had accumulated were obscurely conflicting and combining with each other, and in which the native character of his genius was gradually revealing itself in the new form which it gave to them. The process of accumulation still went on actively—as it went on through all his life—but it now began to be accompanied by a powerful effort to assimilate the matter accumulated, and to change the dead mass of information into the living tissue of thought. Hegel did not, indeed, as he said of Schelling, "carry on his studies in public," and it is only through the publication by his biographer of extracts from his early note-books that we are enabled to get below the rounded utterances of the master to the tentative sketches and imperfect studies of the learner. But no more instructive revelation of the secrets of intellectual growth can be found than in the words, sometimes obscure, but always powerful, and not seldom vividly imaginative, in which Hegel struggles for the expression of a thought which is yet inchoate, and, as it were, in process of germination.

Some of the elements out of which that thought evolved itself have been already mentioned. These were the classical and especially the Greek literature on the one hand, and on the other the so-called *Enlightenment* of the eighteenth century. This *Enlightenment* Hegel had received at first in school in its sober German form, —in the dry analysis and superficial criticism of the post-Wolffian age; but at the university he came to know it in its more intensive French form, which was to the German enlightenment as wine to water. Through Rousseau he proceeded next to Kant's ethical works— following in logical order the evolution of that idea of freedom which was the saving salt of the philosophy of the time. If we further remember that Hegel, educated for the Church, had not as yet ceased to look upon himself as a theologian, we shall not wonder that for several years after this his studies were chiefly directed to the more concrete and practical questions of religion and social ethics, rather than to the abstract metaphysical inquiries which were then mainly occupying the followers of Kant and Fichte. It is also noteworthy that the studies in which he sought for the means of answering these questions were primarily historical rather than philosophical; or became philosophical only through his persistent effort to comprehend and interpret history. At first he was chiefly occupied with the history of religion, and especially with the origin of Christianity, and its connection with the Greek and Jewish religions; and while engaged with this subject he wrote a complete life of Christ, and a treatise on the relation of positive to rational religion. In these and other writings of this period, however, he always considered religion in close relation to the social and political life of nations; and in the Frankfort period, his theological studies gradually connected themselves with extensive inquiries into ethics, political economy, and finally, into the physical and natural sciences. At the same time, this regressive movement of thought, as we may call it, led him to examine more fully the development of philosophy in Kant, Fichte, and Schelling. And in the last year of his stay in Frankfort he finally endeavoured to gather up the result of his investigations in a systematic sketch of philosophy, of which, however, only the Logic and Metaphysic and the Philosophy of Nature were at that time completed.

We may best understand the process of formation through which Hegel's philosophy was going during these six years, if we keep hold of two leading conceptions which were always present to his mind. The one is the idea of freedom or self-determination; the other is the idea of man's life, natural and spiritual, as an organic unity of elements, which cannot be separated from each other without losing all their meaning and value. The former of these was the great principle of the eighteenth century, which was gradually being deepened and transformed in the writings of Rousseau, of Kant, and finally of Fichte. The latter revealed itself to Hegel in the first instance through the religious and political life of Greece. His main difficulty was that these two equally essential ideas seemed to lead in different ways, and to be hardly capable of reconciliation with each other. With this difficulty we find Hegel wrestling in the first writing of his which bears the distinct mark of his genius; and it was the sting, and almost agony, of it which stimulated his unceasing researches in nearly every department of historical and scientific knowledge, and his equally unceasing efforts to penetrate into the inner meaning and uniting principle of the knowledge so acquired. Finally, it was as the solution of this difficulty that the central idea of his philosophy first revealed itself, and it was in constant reference to it that that idea was gradually worked out into a systematic view of the intelligible world in its relation to the intelligence. It is necessary for us, therefore, clearly to understand what these opposite tendencies involved, and how, in the thought of Hegel, they struggled with each other.

The principle of Freedom, as it was first asserted in the Reformation, involved an opposition of the inner to the outer life of man, of conscience to external authority, of the individual as self-determined in all his thought and action to all the influences and objects by which he is, or might be, determined from without. In thrusting aside the claim of the Church to place itself between the individual and God, Luther had proclaimed the emancipation of men not only from the leading-strings of the Church, but, in effect, from all external authority whatever, and even, in a sense, from all merely external teaching or revelation of the truth; for the principle which was announced in the first instance in reference to religion, the central truth of man's being, must inevitably make its way to the circumference, and affect all other elements of his life. If the true knowledge of God be that which comes through the inner witness of the spirit, no other truth can ultimately be accepted in a different way. If the divine law, to which alone absolute submission is due, is revealed by an inward voice, which is one with the voice of our own conscience, no other lawful rule and authority can be merely external. We cannot recognise as *real* any object which is not brought into intelligible relation with our own immediate self-consciousness. We cannot recognise as *just* any command in obeying which we are not obeying our better self. Luther, therefore, had begun a "war of the liberation of humanity," which could not cease until everything foreign and alien, everything that was not seen to form a part of man's own inward life and being, was expelled from all relation to it, and even condemned as meaningless and unreal. *Sub hoc signo vincas.* This is the controlling idea which has ruled the modern movement of civilisation, and the name in which all its great speculative and practical victories have been won.

This principle of freedom was, however, almost necessarily narrowed and distorted by the antagonism in which it first expressed itself. An idea which is used as a weapon of controversy, is on the way to lose its universality and to be turned into a half-truth. Thus the doctrine that nothing ultimately can have authority or even reality for man which is not capable of being made his own and identified with his very self, might be understood to mean that the truth of things is at once revealed to the undeveloped consciousness of the savage or the child, and that the immediate desires of the natural man are his highest law. In place of the duty of knowing for one's self, and of undergoing all the hard discipline, intellectual and moral, which is necessary in order to know, might be put an assertion of the "rights of private judgment," which was equivalent to the proclamation of an anarchy of individual opinion. As the modern struggle for emancipation went on, this ambiguity of the new principle began to reveal itself; and the claims which were first made for the "spiritual man"— *i.e.*, for man in the infinite possibilities of his nature as a rational or self-conscious being, capable of an intellectual and moral life which takes him out of himself, and even of a religious experience which unites him to the infinite,—were reasserted on behalf of the "natural man," *i.e.*, of man conceived merely as a finite individual —an atom set among other atoms in a finite world, and incapable of going beyond it, or even beyond himself, either in thought or action. Hence the strange contradiction which we find in the literature of the eighteenth century, which with one hand exalts the individual almost to a god, while with the other hand it seems to strip off the last veil that hides from him that he is a beast. The practical paradox, that the age in which the claims of humanity were most strongly asserted, is also the age in which human nature was reduced to its lowest terms, —that the age of tolerance, philanthropy, and enlightenment, was also the age of materialism, individualism, and scepticism,—is explicable only if we remember that both equally spring out of the negative form taken by the first assertion of human freedom.

As the individual thus fell back upon himself, throwing off all relations to that which seemed to be external, the specific religious and social ideas of earlier days lost power over him; and their place was taken by the abstract idea of God and the abstract idea of the equality and fraternity of men,—ideas which seemed to be higher and nobler because they were more general, but which for that very reason were emptied of all definite meaning, as well as of all vital power to hold in check the lusts and greeds of man's lower nature. Thus the ambitious but vague proclamation of the religion of nature and the rights of man was closely associated with a theory which was reducing man to a mere animal individual, a mere subject of sensations and appetites, incapable either of religion or of morality. For an ethics which is more than a word, and a religion which is more than an aspiration, imply *definite* relations of men to each other and to God, and all such relations were now rejected as inconsistent with the freedom of the individual. The French Revolution was the practical demonstration that the mere general idea of religion is not a religion, and that the mere general idea of a social unity is not a state, but that such abstractions, inspiring as they may be as weapons of attack upon the old system, leave nothing behind to build up the new one, except the unchained passions of the natural man.

In Rousseau and Kant we find an attempt to develop this abstract principle of freedom into a social system, without altering its abstract or negative character. Rousseau, indeed, saw that the claims made in behalf of the individual must rest on something in him higher than his individual nature. Accordingly, he speaks of a *raison commune* and a *volonté générale*, which is different from the reason and the will of the individuals as such, and which makes them capable of association. But as he regards this universal reason and will merely as a common element in natures which are otherwise unlike each other, and not as a principle which binds them together by means of their very differences, he is unable to develop any organic conception of the social unity. Kant, in like manner, sees in the consciousness of self an element which is common to all men, and which makes community between them possible; and in the idea of self-determination—*i.e.*, of a determination which is conformable to the nature of the self—he finds the principle of all morality. But as he also is unable to show any connection between this general idea and the desires and capacities which determine the particular relations of men to each other and to the world, his morality remains a soul without a body; and it is only by a mystification that he *appears* to be able to get beyond his general principle, and to derive particular laws of duty from it.

Now it is at this point that Hegel takes up the philosophical question. To him, as a son of the Protestant *Aufklärung*, the idea of freedom—the idea that in knowledge and action alike man must be self-determined, that he must find *himself* in the object he knows, and realise *himself* in the end to which he devotes himself—now and always remained axiomatic. In the university, when he was "an enthusiastic champion of liberty and fraternity," he accepted the idea in all the one-sidedness of its first revolutionary expression: and even some years afterwards, we find him writing in the same spirit to Schelling in reference to his account of the Fichtean exaltation of the *ego* over the *non-ego*. "I hold it one of the best signs of the times, that humanity has been presented to its own eyes as worthy of reverence. It is a proof that the nimbus is vanishing from the heads of the oppressors and gods of the earth. Philosophers are now proving the dignity of man, and the people will soon learn to feel it, and not merely to ask humbly for those rights of theirs which have been trampled in the dust, but to resume and appropriate them for themselves." The revolutionary tone which shows itself in these words soon disappeared from Hegel's writing; but to the principle which underlies them—the rejection of any merely external limit to the thoughts and actions of men — he was always faithful, and it was one of the main grounds of his subsequent break with Schelling. And though, in the latter part of his life, Hegel is often supposed to have become politically a reactionary, and though he really did lean to the Conservative side in the immediate politics of Prussia, he never to any degree modified his belief that the principle of liberty is at the root of the political as of all the spiritual life of man. Thus, in one of his latest course of lectures, he declared that Luther, in asserting that each man must find the truth for himself, had laid down the guiding idea of all subsequent history. "Thus was raised the last banner around which the nations gather— the banner of the free spirit, which, in apprehending the truth, still abides with itself, and which, indeed, can only abide by itself as it apprehends the truth. This is the banner under which we serve, and which we carry." If Hegel, then, ever became in any sense an enemy of the *Aufklärung*, it was only on the ground of a deeper interpretation of that principle of freedom which gave the *Aufklärung* its power and value. His controversy with it, like his controversy with Kant and Fichte, was so frequent and unsparing only because he stood so close to it, and even, in a sense, on the very same ground with it. He could afford to be more charitable to those with whom he had less in common.

At the same time, while it is true that Hegel never swerved from the principle of liberty, it is also true that the philosophical impulse was first awakened within him in a recoil against the abstract and one-sided expression of that principle. Already, in the university, he had turned away with weariness from the platitudes of enlightenment. "He who has much to say of the incomprehensible stupidity of mankind, who elaborately demonstrates that it is the greatest folly for a people to have such prejudices, who has always on his tongue the watchwords of 'enlightenment,' 'knowledge of mankind,' 'progress and perfectibility of the species,' &c., is but a vain babbler of the *Aufklärung*, and a vendor of universal medicines,—one who feeds himself with empty words, and ignores the holy and tender web of human affections." Nor is Hegel much better satisfied with the abstract Kantian morality, though he does not yet see his way entirely to reject it. In the same spirit in which Aristotle objected to the Socratic doctrine that "virtue is knowledge," he points out that a real morality implies a habitual temper of mind, which cannot be artificially produced by mere teaching, but must be a living growth of character, evolved from the earliest years by the unconscious influence of a society in which religion, laws, and institutions are all moulded by one spirit. Referring to Kant's admission that a purely rational religion is an impossibility, he objects to his assertion that all that goes beyond the abstract morality of reason, all that is directed to satisfy the feelings and the heart, must be regarded as mere irrational fetich-worship. The feelings after all, Hegel urges, are not so alien to reason as Kant had supposed, "for love is the analogue of reason, in so far as it finds itself in other men; or rather, forgetting itself, finds another self in others in whom it lives, feels, and energises—in the same way that reason, as the principle of universal laws, recognises itself again in every rational being." Hence it is only by acting on the heart and the imagination that a character can be produced which is truly at one with reason; while a morality which addresses the understanding is incapable of any practical effect on the mass of men, and indeed tends to produce an irresolute scrupulous tone of mind which is the reverse of moral strength. "Men who are early bathed in the Dead Sea of moral platitudes come out of it invulnerable like Achilles, but with the human force washed out of them in the process."

What is the source of this violent reaction in Hegel's mind against the Kantian ideas? It is easy to see that the idea of a national religion which should harmonise the imagination and the heart with the reason, was derived by him from Greece. Greek life presented itself to Hegel as a solution of a problem which to Kant had only been approximately soluble,—the problem of combining the universal with the particular, the reason with the feelings. Greek religion was to him the type of a cult which is not merely a combination of rational religion with more or less of fetich-worship, but in which the ceremonial or symbolic element is brought into harmony with the rational. Christianity, on the other hand, he at this time regarded as a moral failure, just because it did not combine with any specific national institutions so as to produce a living development of national character. It was a purely spiritual religion, which sought to influence men through the reason alone, and therefore it remained essentially a religion for individuals. "How light in the scale weigh the whole 'means of grace' worked by the Church, backed by the most full and learned explanations, when the passions, and the power of circumstances, of education, of example, and of the Government, are thrown into the opposite scale! The whole history of religion since the beginning of the Christian era combines to show that Christianity is a religion which can make men good, only if they are good already."

The thought first indicated in this way was followed out, and at once deepened and developed, in a number of theological papers written during Hegel's residence in Switzerland, which might be called "Studies of Jewish and Christian religion from a Greek point of view." Judaism was to Hegel the type of an unnatural religion, a religion of external law, which had no relation to the life of the people on whom it was imposed. The Jews, he maintained, were a nation whose advance from a lower to a higher form of social life had not been a process of natural development, but a violent change forced on them from without. The transition from the simple life of herdsmen to the complex order of the state had not in their case taken place gradually and of itself, but through foreign influence. Driven forward by circumstances and by the ascendancy of a great man, they were forced into a struggle for national independence while yet no real capacity for political life had been formed in them. "Their impulse toward independence was merely a craving for dependence on something of their own;" and therefore, in independence they did not, like other nations, achieve for themselves a noble harmony of natural and spiritual life. They were confined by this narrow patriotism to a bare and almost animal existence, or rose above it only to become the fanatical victims of an abstraction. Their God was not a better self to which their life was drawn up, but an external Lord, whose worship divided them from nature, and even made them hate it. Hence their fate is no Greek tragedy which purifies the passions by terror and pity, for such emotions are called forth only "by the necessary error of a noble character." The Jewish tragedy rather excites horror and disgust, for their fate is "like the fate of Macbeth, who reached beyond nature, allied himself with alien powers, and slavishly worshipped beings not identified with himself; and who, after he had trampled under foot all that was holy in human nature, was necessarily abandoned by his gods, and broken in pieces on the very rock of his own faith."[1]

Hegel then proceeds to compare the idea of law as presented in Judaism with the Greek idea of fate. Law is altogether indifferent to the individual; it fixes limits for him, and attaches to the transgression of those limits a penalty that nothing can avert. There is no possibility of reconciliation with the law; "the soul that sinneth, it shall die,"—and in death there is no reconciliation. On the other hand, the word "fate" takes us into a different and more elevated circle of ideas. A man's fate is immediately connected with his own being; it is something which, indeed, he may fight against, but

[1] Rosenkranz, p. 492.

The Idea of Fate. 27

which is really a part of his own life. Hence, from this point of view, a crime committed by an individual is to be viewed as an outrage upon himself, and the doom which threatens him in consequence is not a mere punishment inflicted by a foreign hand, but the counterpart of his own deed. In slaying his victim, the murderer thinks he has removed an enemy, and enlarged his own life; but really it is one life that is in him and his victim, and in striking at another he has struck at himself. What threatens him, therefore, as his fate, is just his own life made by his deed into a stranger and an enemy. This he cannot slay: it is immortal, and rises from its grave as an awful spectre,—a Clytemnestra which rouses the Eumenides against him; a Banquo's ghost "which is not annihilated by death, but the moment after takes its seat at the banquet, not as a sharer of the meal, but as an evil spirit for Macbeth."

Just this, however, that the penalty is not externally imposed by law, but is simply the fate of the criminal, the recoil of his deed upon himself, makes atonement possible. The guilty conscience of the criminal is his recognition that his own life is in that which he has tried to destroy, and hence it must pass into a longing regret for that which he has thus lost. The criminal, therefore, feels an awe before the fate that weighs upon him, which is quite different from the fear of punishment; for the fear of punishment is the fear of something foreign to him, and the prayers that would avert it are slavish. His fear of fate, on the other hand, is a terror before himself, a consciousness of the agony of divided life, and his prayers to it are not supplications to a master, but rather the beginning of a return to the estranged self. Hence, in this recognition of that which is lost as life, and as his own life, lies the possibility of the complete recovery of it. It is the beginning of that love in which life is restored to itself, and fate is reconciled—in which "the stings of conscience are blunted, and the evil spirit is expelled from the deed."

The idea of fate, however, is not necessarily connected with crime. It is not like the law which only punishes offences against a foreknown command. In the eye of fate *all* action is guilt, for it is necessarily one-sided; it has a special interest or object; it injures other equally vital interests or objects. By the very fact that a man acts, "he enters the arena of combat as power against power," and so subjects himself to fate. Nor by refraining from action can he escape the fate which overtakes the one-sidedness of action. "The valour that struggles is better than the weakness that endures; for though it fails, it knew beforehand the possibility of failure, and consciously made itself liable to it, while suffering passivity is merely caught in its defect, and does not oppose a fulness of energy to it." But neither activity nor passivity can escape its fate. There is, however, still another higher way—a way which combines in one the activity that combats and the patience that endures—the way of Christ, and of all those who have been called "beautiful souls." Such souls follow the path of suffering, in so far as they abandon all their personal rights, and refuse to contend for them; but they pursue also the path of valour, in so far as they rise above this loss of particular right and interest, and feel no pain in it. Thus they save their lives in losing them, or assert themselves just when they let go everything with which immediately their life seemed to be identified. Fate cannot wound such spirits,—for, "like the sensitive plant, they withdraw at a touch into themselves," and escape from the life in which they could be injured. "So Jesus demanded of his friends that they should forsake father and mother, and all that they had, in order that they might not be bound by any tie to the unhallowed world, and so be brought within the reach of fate. 'If any one take thy coat, let him have thy cloak also;' 'If thy right hand offend thee, cut it off.'" Further: "A soul that is thus lifted above all regard for it rights, and disentangled from everything objective, has nothing to forgive to him who injures it. It is ready for reconciliation, capable at once of entering again into vital relations of love and friendship with him;" for whatever he may have done, he cannot have injured it. It has nothing even of that "righteous wrath, that conscientious hate which springs from a sense of wrong, not to the individual, but to justice. For such righteous hate, while it sets up certain duties and rights as absolute, and refuses forgiveness to him who has violated them, takes away from itself the possibility of receiving forgiveness for its own errors, or of being reconciled with the fate that springs from them." Forgiveness of sins, therefore, is not the removal of punishment, for punishment cannot be avoided; nor is it the removal of the consciousness of guilt, for the deed cannot be undone; it is "*fate reconciled by love.*"[1]

On this view, the spirit of Christ is the spirit which withdraws out of the conflict, letting drop every particular interest, and thus, in its universality and freedom,

[1] Rosenkranz, p. 497.

escaping all the claims of the finite. It is reconciled to every fate, and has forgiven every enemy. But just here, as Hegel thinks, lies its limit and imperfection. "Jesus has the *guilt of innocency*, and his elevation above every fate brings with it the most unhappy of fates." The meaning of this somewhat obscure utterance is, that as Christ purchased reconciliation by withdrawing out of the sphere in which private interests and rights conflict with each other, his very negation of these becomes a limit to him. All sides are against him who does not strike for any side. Priest and magistrate, Pharisee and Sadducee, unite against him who is above their divisions, and does not recognise as vital any of the interests for which they are contending. His very withdrawal from the sphere of battle is the source of a more bitter hostility, and makes his people reject him, and turn from his doctrine to a desperate struggle for the narrow ideal of national life. His teaching, indeed, is eagerly accepted by other men who have no share in the fate of the Jewish nationality; but with them, too, it remains incapable of being brought into unity with any of the finite interests of life. The unity of love reached by the negation of all particular rights and duties remains incapable of expansion into any new order of secular life; and as it cannot become the principle of the life of the world, it is obliged to fall back on the spiritual unity of the Church—a society of men withdrawn from the world, and living solely for this concentrated life of devotional feeling. "Beyond the relation that arises out of the common faith, and the manifestation of this community in appropriate religious acts, the Christian Church remains incapable of any objective aim—incapable of co-

Christianity. 31

operation for any other end than the spread of the faith, and incapable of finding expression or satisfaction in any of the various manifestations and partial forms of our manifold life. For in following any other direction, it could not recognise itself: it would have forsaken the pure love which is its sole spirit, and have become untrue to its God. This limitation of love to itself,—this flight from all forms, even if its own spirit were breathing in them,—this removal from all fate, is its greatest fate; and this is the point at which Jesus is connected with fate, and, in the sublimest way indeed, suffers from it." Hence, also, the ever-dubious attitude of the Church to the world, never able either to divide itself from it—since love is supposed to be the universal principle; nor to reconcile itself with it—for love is not able to enter into its particular and finite relations. "Between the extremes of friendship, hate, and indifference to the world, the Christian consciousness has gone backwards and forwards; but it is its fate that Church and State, divine service and life, piety and virtue, can never for it melt into one."

The result is, then, that Christianity produces, or indicates, an unhealthy division between religion and life. It does not solve the problem, which, in its way, the Greek religion, inasmuch as it simply idealised the actual forces of the political life, proved itself competent to solve. "To the Greek, the idea of his fatherland, his State, was the invisible, the higher reality, for which he laboured, and which formed his persistent motive. This was his end and aim of the world, or the end and aim of *his* world, which he found expressed in reality, and which he himself helped to express and to maintain.

In comparison with this idea, his own individuality was as nothing: it was *its* endurance—*its* continued life—that he sought, and this he was himself able to realise. To desire or pray for permanence or eternal life for himself as an individual, could not occur to him; or, at least, it was only in moments of inaction and despondency that he could feel a stronger wish and relation to his individual self. Cato did not turn for comfort to Plato's "Phædo," till that which had hitherto been for him the highest order of things—*his* world, his republic—was destroyed: then only did he take refuge in a yet higher order." Religion, in short, was to the ancients simply the idealisation of the actual powers of man's life—of the higher passions that moved him—of the ideal interests of the social and political life in which he lived. Rome, however, in conquering the nations, put an end to this religion of free citizens, whose highest was within their own grasp. It turned the State from an organic unity of life, which took up into itself the whole being of its citizens, into a dead mechanism of government, externally applied to a powerless mass of subjects. "Then death must have become terrible to the citizen, because nothing of his own survived him; whereas the republic survived the republican, and he could cherish the thought that it—his soul—was eternal." After this time, greater demands began to be made upon religion, and the imperfect human-like gods, which had been sufficient for the imagination so long as human life itself was so full of divinity, could no longer satisfy the cravings of the spirit. "The spirit of man could not cease to seek *somewhere* for the absolute, for independence, for power; and as this was no longer to be met with in the will of man, it had to be found in the God of Christianity—a God who was lifted beyond the sphere of the powers and will of man, yet not beyond reach of his prayers and cries; for the realisation of a moral idea could now only be wished,— it could no longer be willed." The divine kingdom, however, which, it was at first hoped, would be realised immediately, had soon to be put off to the end of the world. " In fact, so soon as the realisation of an idea is put beyond the limits of human power, it does not matter how far off it is placed; and the further it was removed, with the more wonderful colours could it be painted by the oriental imagination." But this separation of God from man has had fatal effects. "The objectivity of God has gone hand in hand with the slavery and corruption of man." While there was a living organisation of society, the social life of man was itself regarded as a manifestation of the divine, and God was simply the better self of His worshippers; but when national life disappeared, and the Church took the place of the State, man became in his own eyes a *non-ego*, and his God was another. "It has been left for our day," says Hegel, in the spirit of some of his later followers of the Left, " to challenge again as the property of man the treasures that were formerly squandered upon heaven—to challenge them at least in theory. But what age will have the courage and energy to make this right a reality, and to set man actually in possession of his own?"[1]

We see here the compromise between the different tendencies contending within him, in which Hegel for the time found satisfaction. On the one hand he holds

[1] Haym, p. 474 *et seq.*

to the principle of freedom, and echoes the latest interpretation of it by Fichte, who at this time regarded the choice between idealism and realism—between the doctrine that the *ego* produces the *non-ego*, and the doctrine that the *non-ego* produces the *ego*—as a test of moral character. A quite consistent philosophy, Fichte allowed, might be developed in both ways, both on the realist and on the idealist hypothesis; but he who was free in spirit would find the explanation of the world in freedom, and he who was a slave at heart would find it in necessity. Hegel, in the main, accepts this language of Fichte, but he does not draw the line between self and not-self at the point where Fichte draws it. To Fichte as to Kant, the State was still an external combination of individuals, a thing of outward order, while morality was confined entirely to the inner life. But to Hegel, filled with the spirit of Greek literature, the social life of the State could not be a thing external or indifferent to the moral life of the individual; rather it was the truer self, in which and for which the individual was bound to live, and with which he was so intimately identified that, while *it* survived, he need not think of any personal immortality. It was only outside of this intimate circle that the "cold world" lay, which was really external and objective. Hence Hegel did not regard the Greek political life as involving any sacrifice of the freedom of the individual, but rather as the realisation of that freedom; and Greek religion was to him a "subjective" religion, whose gods only imaginatively and for a moment drew their worshipper away from the centre of his own life, but were immediately recognised as powers that are working in his own will and thought. It is only to Christianity—which he regards as a religion of pure undeveloped love, and, therefore, as a religion of the other world—that Hegel applies the Fichtean condemnation of an "objective" religion, a worship of the *non-ego*, a religion inconsistent with the freedom of man. Hence he describes the revolt against Christianity and the new idealistic philosophy as a reclaiming for man of the treasures he has lavished upon God; and in a poem addressed to Hölderlin, Hegel declares that the desecrated altars of Eleusis are being reared again by the initiated in their own hearts. How the new revival was to differ from the old Greek type, he does not say. Christianity, at least, he seems at this time to regard as essentially bound up with the medieval dualism, and therefore as not containing in itself the principle of a new life.

The transition from this to a higher point of view seems to have taken place in the beginning of Hegel's residence at Frankfort, and in connection with a remarkable change of language which we find in his papers written about that time. In Switzerland he had used the words "life" and "love" to express the highest kind of social unity; now he substitutes the word "spirit." This is no mere verbal change. The word "life" suggests the idea of an organic unity, and the word "love" implies that the members of that unity are conscious beings— conscious of the social organism in which they merge their separate existence, and conscious also of themselves, were it only in the moment of self-surrender by which they give themselves up to that organism. In these terms, therefore, Hegel found a means of expressing that social unity of which the Greek State was to him the type—a unity of individuals who regarded themselves not as isolated persons, but simply as citizens whose life was in the State, and who had no personality apart from it. In such a social unity the idea of self is involved, but it is not emphasised; the division of self-conscious individuals disappears like the separateness of notes in a harmony.

"Love took up the harp of life, and smote on all the chords
 with might,
Smote the chord of self, which, trembling, passed in music
 out of sight."

But the term "spirit," or "spiritual unity," seems to convey—and in Hegel's language always conveys— the idea of antagonism overcome, contradiction reconciled, unity reached through the struggle and conflict of elements, which, in the first aspect of them, are opposed to each other. It was, therefore, the appropriate expression for a unity between the mind and the object which is contrasted with it,—between mind and matter,—or between different self-conscious subjects, each of whom has a complete consciousness of his own independent rights and personality. Such a unity can never be, in Hegel's language, *immediate*—*i.e.*, can never be ready-made from the first, but always involves a process by which difference is overcome, and opposition transformed into agreement. Nor can this be a merely *natural* process—*i.e.*, a process in which the opposition melts away without being heard of. Rather it is a process which begins with a distinct consciousness of independence to be renounced, of opposition to be over-

The Idea of Spirit.

come, and which involves, therefore, an explicit surrender of independence, a conscious reconciliation of the opposition.

This use of the term "spirit," in fact, indicates that the Greek ideal was becoming unsatisfactory to Hegel, as being an incomplete solution of his primary difficulty of the connection of the universal and particular. Hitherto Hegel's criticism of Kant's abstract opposition of reason and passion had been practically this,—that though diverse they were capable of coincidence, and that the Greeks had actually solved the problem of harmonising them. But the unity so attained was, as Hegel now saw, exceptional and transitory, the product of specially favourable circumstances and of a peculiar national genius. For the Greek State, and the ethical harmony of life realised in it, could be regarded only as the creation of a people of artists, which, by a combination of skill and good fortune, had for once moulded the untoward matter of human existence into a political work of art. But such an achievement, like other works of art, is valuable mainly as an earnest of something more universal. "Poetic justice" is an exceptional thing out of poetry, because, in the entanglement of human affairs, we cannot easily find a small circle of events which forms a whole by itself, and in which the ideal law is clearly revealed. But the value of the exception is that it points to such a law. Beauty is an accidental or momentary coincidence of the universal and the particular, of understanding and sense, and an earnest of their complete reconciliation. If, however, we are to apply the idea of organic unity to the world,—if we are to regard man as capable of achieving such a unity in his own life,—we cannot be satisfied with such a partial and accidental meeting of ideal and real, of the inner and the outer life. We must not think of man as struggling with an external power which occasionally yields him a partial victory. We must be able to see that there is a harmony or unity between the inward and the outward which is deeper than all their antagonism, and which is realising itself even when that antagonism seems to be greatest. It must be shown not merely that the *ego* gains an occasional victory over the *non-ego*, but that, in spite of all their apparent opposition, it is one principle which is manifesting itself in *non-ego* and *ego* alike. If, therefore, the idea of organic unity was to be used, as Hegel sought to use it, to supplement and correct the abstract idea of freedom expressed by Kant and Fichte, it was necessary to give it a more extended and difficult application than Hegel had hitherto attempted. It was no longer enough for him to say that there are organisms in the world—natural and spiritual organisms—but the whole world must be conceived as itself an organism. That poetic or artistic products exist or are achieved by man both in art and in life was no longer all that was wanted: it was necessary that all nature and history should be seen to have the unity of a poem.

But obviously this new demand involves far greater difficulties than have yet been considered. If all the world is to be conceived as poetic,—ἡ τοῦ βίου σύμπασα τραγῳδία καὶ κωμῳδία,—our poetry must find room for much which to the immediate eye of imagination is unpoetic and vulgar. If nature is to be taken as an organism, it must at least be recognised that it has parts in

The Idea of Spirit.

it which, regarded in themselves, are inorganic. If all things are members in a living whole, the life that animates that whole must have a wider definition,—it must be a life which comprehends even death itself. Pain, disharmony, and evil, must be seen to be incapable of breaking through the all-embracing unity, and even to be themselves the means of realising it. Unreason itself must find a place, were it only a place to annihilate itself, under the universal rule of reason, which impartially rains its fertilising showers upon the evil and the good, and stimulates each in turn to show what is in it; since just in this impartiality lies the security for the triumph of good. In such a theory optimism must be reached not by the exclusion but by the exhaustion of pessimism: the ultimate affirmation of philosophy must include in itself and overcome all the negations and contradictions of scepticism.

At first it would seem as if the problem so stated must be regarded as insoluble; for what is required is no less than to find a principle of unity adequate to the reconciliation of the strongest antagonisms and contradictions which language can express. And is not this almost like asking that words should be deprived of all their meaning? Yet, on the other hand, *if* the world is to be conceived as a rational system, *if* the particular is to be combined in organic unity with the universal, *if* man is in any sense to be regarded as free in spite of the limiting conditions under which nature seems to bring him, the discovery of such a principle is a necessity. Fichte, against his will, proved that it is impossible to view the inner life of the subject as a rational system in itself, unless the object also were brought within the compass of that system. He tried, indeed, to escape this necessary consequence by treating the connection of the *ego* with the *non-ego* as a purely negative relation. But a negative relation is still a relation. The self is bound up in one whole with that not-self to which it is opposed, and unless *that* also can be regarded as in some sense rational, there can be no rational system at all.

Hegel seems at first to have faltered before the problem of philosophy thus presented to him, and to have felt inclined to take refuge from its difficulty—as Schelling afterwards took refuge—in a religious intuition or feeling of the unity of all things,—an intuition to which thought might lead up, but in which its activity must disappear. In other words, he seems to have held for a short time that reason is unable itself to rise above the oppositions and contradictions of things, though it is able to see that there *is* a limit to such oppositions, and that there *is* an absolute unity lying beyond them. "Philosophy must end in religion, because philosophy is thought, and thought always involves finitude and opposition,—*e.g.*, the oppositions of subject and object, and of the mind that thinks to matter that does not think. Its business, therefore, is to show the finitude of all that is finite, and through reason to demand its complement or completion in the infinite." [1]

But this solution seems to have been only a moment of transition in Hegel's philosophical development. If reason can discern that there *is* a unity in which all difference is lost, it must be able to see what that unity is; for the perception of limits is possible only to one who can see beyond them. The reason that looks through

[1] Rosenkranz, p. 96.

The Idea of Spirit. 41

all oppositions of things to their unity, must be able to grasp that unity and to cast the light of it upon these very oppositions. If even Schelling could not rest in the assertion that the artistic or religious intuition is the highest apprehension of truth, but was driven, with some inconsequence, to attempt to reconstruct the world from the point of view so reached, still less could Hegel be content to view philosophy as a process which ends in the absolute unity, and does not give rise to any new consciousness of finite things in relation to that unity. And the word which was to be the key-note of this new interpretation of things *sub specie æternitatis* has already been named. The world may still be conceived as an organic unity, in spite of its extreme division and antagonism, because it is *spiritual*, or the revelation of spirit. For a spiritual unity is a unity which can endure the extremest antagonism and conflict—nay, it is a unity which can be realised only through such conflict. The very existence of a spirit is a perpetual proof of the unity of opposites. When we consider how a spiritual being grows and realises itself, we see that it is by a perpetual process of self-denial. *Intellectually* it can develop its powers only by going out of itself; by yielding to impressions from without; by persistently occupying itself with the not-self—the world of objects; and without such occupation with the external, it could not even be conscious of itself. And if we regard the *practical* life of such a being, we have to give a similar account of it. For all moral growth consists in learning to go out of self, and so to take a wider life into our own. It begins, therefore, in the negation of immediate desires and appetites which, if they were suffered directly to assert themselves, would assuredly defeat their own ends. It is only as the individual gets beyond such particular impulses, and forms in himself a will which has regard to something more general,—a will which acts from the point of view of the family, of the state, or of humanity, or at least a will which looks to some objective interest or end,—that he can be said to have a will of his own at all. Spiritual life is thus essentially a process of transcending and overcoming those very oppositions which seem to be of the most intense and absolute character—the oppositions of subject and object, mind and matter, internal and external; it is, in the Kantian phrase, a "nest of contradictions," and yet this does not destroy its unity with itself. If, therefore, we regard the ultimate unity as a spiritual principle, there is good hope that we may find in it a key to the antagonism and conflict of things, and may be enabled to see in the world not a mere wilderness and chaos of opposing powers, or the Manichæan dualism of an absolute good and an absolute evil, but a rational order or system, an organic unity in which every member has its place and function.

Such a system we find Hegel seeking to develop for himself in the years 1799-1800, the last two years of his residence in Frankfort. The peculiarities of this first outline of his philosophy it is unnecessary here to consider: what has been already said may be sufficient to show that in it Hegel was now seeking to develop his characteristic idea, that the highest unity is to be reached only through the full development and reconciliation of the deepest and widest antagonism. Some such conception was already involved in the threefold movement of thought by thesis, antithesis, and synthesis, which had been suggested by Kant, and developed, though in a somewhat imperfect and external way, by Fichte and Schelling. Hegel distinguishes himself from both, even in this early sketch, by the firmness with which he grasps the idea of the unity of opposites, not as an external synthesis, but as a result of the necessary evolution of thought by means of an antagonism which thought itself produces and reconciles. The further explanation of this process must, however, be postponed till a later chapter. Here it need only be remarked that Hegel has already, though with some hesitation and uncertainty, marked out the general threefold division of his system, which corresponds to the three elements or movements just mentioned. The first part of the system consists of a Logic and a Metaphysic—which, however, are not yet completely identified by Hegel, as they were at a later period; the second is a Philosophy of Nature; and the third, which was not worked out in the Frankfort sketch, is the Philosophy of Spirit.

One other point, the full consideration of which must also be reserved for a future chapter, may be mentioned here. It is that, with the rise of this new idea of spirit as the unity of all differences, Hegel's attitude towards Christianity was completely changed. For in the central moral principle of Christianity, the principle of self-realisation through self-sacrifice, he found just that movement through negation to affirmation, through opposition to reconciliation, which he was seeking. Or rather, perhaps we should say that it was Hegel's study of Christianity, assisted by the contemporary development of philosophy, which first suggested to him the idea of that movement. Hence if we should seek to gather up the Hegelian philosophy in a sentence, as a Frenchman once asked Hegel to do, it would be this: that the words "die to live" express not only the dialectic of morals, but the universal principle of philosophy. For if these words truly express the nature of spiritual life, then in spirit may be found a unity which will account for and overcome all the antagonisms of life and thought. The full meaning of this statement, however, is not to be seen without many explanations which cannot as yet be given.

CHAPTER III.

HEGEL AND SCHELLING—JENA, 1800-1807.

During the long mental struggle, the history of which has been outlined in the last chapter, Hegel had in the main lived for himself, without any attempt to communicate his thoughts to the world. When he visited his family at Stuttgart, on his way from Switzerland to Frankfort, his sister found that he had become silent and self-absorbed; and about the same time Schelling wrote to reproach him with yielding to a kind of irresolution and dejection of spirit that was unworthy of him. A depressed, melancholic, almost sentimental tone, unusual with Hegel, runs through the somewhat ill-constructed verses—he had not a good ear for metre—specimens of which his biographer has published. The only literary work which he prepared for the press during the Frankfort period, was an essay on the reforms in the constitution of his native Würtemberg, the necessity of which had been made evident by the rough pressure of France: and even this was not published. In philosophical matters, the conflict of opposing thoughts and sympathies of which he was not yet master kept him silent. But now, in the year 1800, when he had at last grasped the leading idea of his system, and had commenced to work out its application with some degree of systematic fulness, he began to long for an opportunity of expressing himself, and of comparing his thoughts with those of others. In this view he reopened communication with Schelling, with whom his correspondence had apparently dropped for some years, and informed his friend that he was prepared, or rather that he was almost prepared, to take his share in the philosophical battle. Hegel's father had died in the beginning of 1799, and the small sum of about £300 which he had received as his share of the family inheritance, made him for a time independent of the work of teaching. Accordingly, in his letter to Schelling, he begs him to recommend some economical place of residence,—he would prefer a Catholic city, in order to have a nearer view of that religion, — where he could live cheaply (with, as he specially states, the advantage of *ein gutes Bier*), enjoy some good society, and gather himself together before entering into the literary and philosophical hubbub of Jena. He has, he declares, watched Schelling's great public career " with admiration and joy," but wishes Schelling to know that *he himself* also has been in silence making his way to a philosophical view of things. " In my scientific education, which began with the endeavour to satisfy humbler wants, I have been driven onward to philosophy, and *the ideal of youth has thus, of necessity, had to take on the form of reflection, and transform itself into a system.* Now, while I am still employed with this task, I begin to ask myself where I can find a point of contact to bring my thoughts to bear upon human life. Of all the men I see around me, you are the one in whom I should most desire to find a friend, as in other things, so especially in reference to this business of getting myself expressed, and brought into effective contact with the world; for I see that you have apprehended man as he is—*i.e.*, with a comprehensive sympathy which is unstained by vanity. I therefore can look to you with the full confidence that you will be able to recognise my disinterested endeavours, and to find a value in them."

In this appeal to Schelling there is traceable a wish on Hegel's part to indicate to his friend that he is *substantially*, though only substantially, at one with him, and that though for this reason he can hope to co-operate with Schelling, yet that the philosophical form which his thoughts have taken has grown by an independent process out of the needs of his own spirit. When we consider how Hellenic art and life had been to Hegel the first key to the spiritual significance of things, how the idea of organic unity derived from that source had gradually transformed itself under the influence of philosophical criticism, and how, finally, by the aid of the idea of spirit, it had been applied, not merely to the State, but to the world as a whole,—the special words of this announcement will seem significant and characteristic. The answer of Schelling is not preserved; but the result was that Hegel gave up the idea of a preliminary retreat to Bamberg or any other city, and resorted at once, in January 1801, to Jena, to take his place beside Schelling as a champion of "the philosophy of Identity." In July of the same year appeared his first published work, 'On the Difference between the Systems of Fichte and Schelling,' in which Hegel appears as in all essential points a defender of the latter against the former. The dissertation 'De orbitis planetarum,' which he published immediately afterwards, *pro licentia docendi*, and which was written very much in the spirit of Schelling's Philosophy of Nature, though on a subject which Schelling had never discussed, confirmed the idea of Hegel's complete agreement with Schelling; and he had soon after to contradict the statement of a newspaper that he was a fellow-Würtemberger whom Schelling had brought forward under his wing, to be a special pleader in his behalf. But though asserting his own independence with decision and almost with violence, Hegel was at this time quite willing to accept the place of a defender of the philosophy of Identity; and in 1802 he united with Schelling in the publication of a 'Critical Journal,' in which the contributions of the two writers were not in any way distinguished from each other—a circumstance which, after Hegel's death, led to some controversy about the authorship of several of the pieces.

The common point of view which is expressed in this Journal, as well as in Hegel's treatise and Schelling's successive works of this period, is, as has been said, that of the so-called "philosophy of Identity." This may be better understood if we remember to what it was opposed. It was opposed, on the one hand, to that common-sense dualism for which mind and matter, or subject and object, are two things absolutely independent of each other—two things which, if brought into relation at all, can only be externally harmonised, like the two clocks of Leibnitz, but between which no kindred nature or principle of unity can be discovered. In like manner, it was opposed to the Kantian and the Fichtean

Fichte and Schelling.

philosophy of subjectivity, which, indeed, had expressed the idea of a unity beyond difference—a unity of subject and object, perception and thought—but which had not fully developed that idea, or had developed it only in a partial and subjective way. Thus, in the Kantian philosophy, only the phenomenal object was supposed to be knowable, while the real object was treated as a thing-in-itself—*i.e.*, a thing not essentially related to, or knowable by, the subject; and, on the other hand, the subject was regarded as incapable of reaching beyond his own sensations and impulses—beyond the circle of his own inner life, so as to know or to act on anything but himself. In the Fichtean philosophy, again, the independent existence of things in themselves, outside of the circle of subjective phenomena, was denied; and the *non-ego* was reduced to a negative condition, through which the *ego* realises its own life of self-determination: nay, even this negative condition, the *ego*, by an incomprehensible act, was supposed to produce for, and out of, itself. But the effect of this theory of Fichte was, not to idealise the object, but rather to explain it away, and to confine the *ego* to a mere inward struggle with itself, in which it could never go beyond itself in a real self-surrender, and therefore could never return to itself with the fruit of a real liberty. The *non-ego* was thus reduced by Fichte to a spectre: but, in spite of that, or just because of that, it could never be vanquished or spiritualised. If it ceased to exist as an outward object, it was only to reappear as an incomprehensible opposition of the mind to itself. Schelling made the first step out of this charmed circle of subjectivity, when he endeavoured to show that in nature there is the same movement of antagonism and reconciliation as in spirit: in other words, that nature also has in it a dualism corresponding to the dualism of self and not-self in consciousness, and that therefore it is *one* principle which we find manifested in mind and matter alike. To Fichte's declaration that "the I is everything," he adds, therefore, the converse that "everything is I"—*i.e.*, that nature is no unreal shadow of the movement of subjective thought, but has manifested in it the very principle which constitutes the *ego* in man. Hence, as Schelling expressed it—and Hegel for a time made no objection to the expression—there are no qualitative, but only quantitative, differences in things. Each of the two opposites, mind and matter, is in itself a subject-object, and contains and reconciles in itself the opposition of an ideal and a real element. And the same is true of every separable form, whether of mind or matter; so that, from the point of view of the absolute, everything that exists is an identity of subject and object, and all these identities are essentially one.

The essential principle, then, in which Hegel and Schelling meet together, is that there is a unity which is above all differences, which maintains itself through all differences, and in reference to which all differences must be explained. They agree also in calling this unity spiritual, and in asserting it as the *articulus stantis vel cadentis philosophiæ*—the point of view at which all true philosophy must place itself in order to understand the world. The programme of the 'Critical Journal' asserts, therefore, that "the great immediate interest of philosophy is to put God again absolutely at the head of the system as the one ground of all, the *principium essendi et cognos-*

cendi, after He has been for a long time placed, either as one finitude alongside of other finitudes, or at the end of them all as a postulate,—which necessarily implies the absoluteness of the finite." In other words, philosophy has hitherto started with some fixed opposition, such as those of subject and object, of mind and matter, of freedom and necessity, forgetting that these oppositions could not be intelligible except on the presupposition of a unity that transcends them. Now this presupposed unity, "just because it is *presupposed*, is not present to the ordinary consciousness, which, therefore, always thinks of the object as essentially different from the subject." It is an unconsciously assumed basis of consciousness, which philosophy brings to light, and by aid of which it transforms our ordinary view of the world. Hence, also, scepticism performs a valuable service to philosophy, in that it confuses and destroys the distinctions of the ordinary consciousness, or exhibits their relative and limited character. Thus, when the popular consciousness (or the common-sense philosophy which makes itself the spokesman of that consciousness), asserts that the object and the subject of knowledge are essentially distinct, scepticism points out that knowledge, as involving their relation to each other, is inconsistent with such distinctness. In other words, scepticism proves, on the hypothesis of the distinction of subject and object, that knowledge is impossible. But the true conclusion from this argument is, that the object is *not* absolutely distinct from the subject that knows it, but in its distinctness is yet essentially related to, and so one with, it. The negative dialectic of the sceptic, therefore, proves only that each limited idea contains its own negation, and thus carries us back to that identity which is presupposed in all distinction, and in the light of which each distinction is reduced to its proper meaning and value, as a manifestation or expression of the unity.

To Schelling and Hegel it appeared that this idea of the unity beyond all differences was the new inspiring principle which was to liberate science and life from the bonds of abstraction in which they had been hitherto held. The Cartesian dualism, with its abstract opposition of mind to matter, had, they asserted, only given philosophical expression to the principle of an all-embracing dualism, which was already manifesting itself in the political and religious life of Europe in the breaking up of the old feudal and Catholic system. On this principle of division, and therefore of death, all the sciences had been based, and they had therefore been built up into "a temple of the understanding which reason had deserted." Now at last the literature of the time was beginning to show a weariness of this shallow *expansion*, this accumulation of dead facts, to which the spiritual bond was wanting. A longing had been awakened, as it were "a thirst of Dives for a drop of fire"—a curious metaphor—"for a concentration of living intuition," which might destroy the divisions of reflection, and reveal again the organic unity of the world. It was the business of the philosophical critics to assist in the development of this new consciousness, to carry on vigorously the war against the dualistic dogmatism and scepticism of common-sense, to recognise and appreciate every manifestation, however imperfect, of the great idea of Identity or Unity, and to disentangle it from the imperfections of its expression.

In the former point of view, the Journal proposes to carry fire and sword into the quarters of writers like Schulz, Krug, and even Reinhold, who held by the fixed oppositions of the finite as if they were absolute; in the latter point of view, it proposes to apply a discriminating criticism to the mystics—"the beautiful souls"—who had apprehended "the pure idea of philosophy" without being able to give it scientific expression, and also to the theories of Kant, Fichte, and their followers, in which that idea was present, though in a one-sided and still preponderantly subjective form. For these philosophers, just because of their leaning to the subjective as opposed to the objective, had "not broken through to pure formlessness, or, what is the same thing, to the absolute form;"—*i.e.*, they had not, by equal negation of *all* differences, reached the unity in which all distinction and differentiation begin, the universal point of view from which alone particulars can be truly estimated and understood.

The articles in the Journal were unsigned, to indicate the unity of spirit in the authors; but it was mainly by Hegel that this programme, especially the latter part of it, was carried out, even if we give Schelling the benefit of the doubt in all cases in which the authorship of the different pieces is uncertain. Schelling, indeed, soon directed his main literary activity to a new 'Journal for Speculative Physics,' which he established, leaving the work of the 'Critical Journal' to Hegel. Schelling's removal from Jena in the summer of 1803, which put an end to the intimate alliance of the two friends, may have had something to do with the cessation of the latter Journal. It is, however, clear, that closely as they were asociated in their polemical work, Schelling and Hegel were certain to diverge from each other as soon as an advance was made to a positive definition and evolution of the principle of "identity." And this divergence is already manifested in the essay which constitutes the last number of the Journal, in which Hegel retracts the admission of the equality of nature and spirit made in his first treatise, and asserts that, as the absolute unity or identity is *spiritual*, so spirit "overreaches" nature, or includes it as a factor in its own life.

The truth is, that the 'Critical Journal' indicates a point of coincidence between two minds that were advancing in somewhat different directions. Schelling, on his side, had never quite freed himself from the Fichtean idea, according to which the *ego* and the *non-ego*, or the two factors that correspond to them in nature, are fundamentally irreconcilable. Hence, when he spoke of the absolute as the identity in which all such difference and opposition is transcended, he was not able to think of it as still leaving room for the play of difference, but was inclined rather to conceive it as an absolute oneness, in which all division and distinction is submerged and lost. In this spirit he declared that the finite is explicable only from itself, but not from the infinite, and spoke of the organ of philosophy as an "intellectual intuition," analogous to the sensuous intuition of the artist, but entirely opposed to "reflection," —*i.e.*, to all thought which moves by reasoning from part to part, and does not grasp the whole at once in one comprehensive glance of genius. While, therefore, he agreed with Hegel in calling the unity *spiritual*, and in conceiving it as a unity of subject and object, of knowing and being, yet he emphasised the unity at the expense of the difference, and had much more success in showing that *they* all disappear in *it*, than that *it* can in any way reproduce *them* from itself. And when he proceeded to develop his system, he seemed externally to take up again the finite elements he had rejected, rather than to develop them with a new meaning from the principle. His unity, therefore, as Hegel afterwards said, was a unity of "substance" rather than of spirit; or if it was nominally spiritual, yet the idea of spirit, if it be left undifferentiated and undeveloped, is little more than the idea of substance.

Now it is observable that in all these respects Hegel distinguished himself from Schelling even at the time when they were most closely allied. In the treatise "On the Difference of the Fichtean and Schellingian Systems," he insists that the identity of philosophy is not an abstract identity as opposed to difference, but a spiritual unity which differentiates itself, that through opposition and conflict it may reach a higher unity. "The necessary diremption is one factor of the life which forms itself by eternal opposition; and the totality, which is in the highest sense vital or organic, is produced only by restoration out of the most extreme division." Hence the true "intellectual intuition" is not an immediate apprehension of truth which is exclusive of the process of reflection, but includes that process in itself. At the same time, Hegel still holds with Schelling that the movement of reflection *outside* of philosophy is quite different from its movement *within* it; and that the highest result to be achieved by the former is the *felo de se* of scepticism,—*i.e.*, to carry up the finite categories to self-contradiction, and so *negatively* prepare the way for the intuition of the absolute identity. Philosophy, therefore, in spite of this negative introduction, is regarded as starting, in Spinozistic fashion, with the absolute. "As an objective totality, knowledge furnishes the reason or ground for itself, and its parts are grounded at the same time as the whole. It is thus a whole which has no more need of a special handle in the way of an external reason through which it may be proved, than the earth needs a special handle to be grasped by the force that carries it round the sun." Hence Hegel is very severe in his criticism of Reinhold, who would begin by hypothetically assuming some relative point of view, and making his way from it to the principle of philosophy. On the contrary, argues Hegel, there is *no way* from the finite to the infinite; we can only reach the latter if we deny and cast loose from the former. The only way to get entrance into philosophy is to throw in one's self headlong "*à corps perdu hineinzustürzen.*" Reinhold's philosophy, just because it begins with preliminaries outside of philosophy, never gets beyond preliminaries—"the whole of his force is wasted in the run, and nothing is left for the leap." In an amusing squib, written against Reinhold, Schelling refers to this criticism upon hypothetical philosophy, and speaks of Hegel as "a downright categorical kind of being, who tolerates no ceremony with philosophy, but, without waiting for any such grace before meat, falls to at once with a good appetite."

It is, however, just at this point that we find one of the germs of division between Hegel and Schelling. Hegel's denial of the need of an introduction to philosophy is ambiguous, for the negative propædeutic of sceptical reflection which he admits is still an introduction. Reinhold's real fault was not that he started with the finite, and made his way from it to the infinite, but that he did not see that it is through the negation of the former that we reach the latter. It is because the finite—if we take it as an absolute independent existence—contradicts itself, that we are driven back upon the infinite. On the other hand, this process is not purely negative, but has in it a positive element which Schelling, and Hegel also at this time, seemed to neglect. It is not simply that, by the self-negation of the finite, room is made for the intuitive genius of the philosopher to grasp the infinite. The negative attitude toward the finite involves in itself an inchoate consciousness of the infinite; "we are near awaking when we dream that we dream." Or, to put the matter in a different point of view, the ordinary consciousness, because it is in its way a thinking consciousness, carries in *itself* the means of its own correction; and philosophy, in refuting and transforming it, is yet bound to pay it due respect *as* a thinking consciousness, and to refute it out of its own mouth. If the philosopher does otherwise,—if he assumes prophetic airs, or speaks to ordinary men from the height of an "immediate insight" or "transcendental intuition," from which they are excluded,—he, as Hegel soon began to assert, is pretending "to be of a different species from other men," and is "trampling the roots of humanity under foot." Besides, in doing so he is actually abandoning his highest claim, which consists simply in this, that he is not speaking like an artist to those who have some special natural gift or taste, but is interpreting that universal consciousness which is in all rational beings as such, and which, therefore, all are capable of recognising. "If philosophy requires of the individual that he should lift himself into the pure ether of thought, on the other hand the individual has a right to demand of philosophy that it should let down a ladder on which he may ascend to this point of view; nay, that it should show him that he has already this ladder in his own possession. This right is founded upon the absolute independence which, in every form of consciousness, be its content what it may, a rational being knows himself to possess; for in every such form there is involved the immediate certitude of self-consciousness—a consciousness which is not conditioned by anything out of itself."[1] In other words, a rational being, because he is rational, has a right to demand that the highest truth shall be presented to him not as a revelation of something foreign and strange, but as the explanation of that which already he is conscious of being.

The mistake of Schelling, in absolutely opposing philosophy to the reflective thought of the finite consciousness, had another bad effect. It produced a neglect of method in philosophy itself. Relying on "intellectual intuition," and seeing in everything the manifestation of one principle, Schelling and his followers represented the world as a series of "potencies" of the absolute; but in doing so, they rather externally fitted the threefold schema of Kant to the given matter of the sciences, than developed the particulars out of

[1] Hegel, ii. 20.

the general principle. At most they moved by vague analogies, by poetic leaps and bounds, rather than by any definite process or evolution of thought. They did not do sufficient justice to the different elements of experience really to overcome their differences, and bring them back to unity. While, therefore, their negative dialectic simply blotted out all the difference of finite things, and merged them in the absolute, their positive dialectic, if it could be called dialectic, was a series of superficial analogies, or, at best, happy guesses, which might be guided by a true idea, but which did not really bring that idea into living contact with the special characteristics of each sphere of reality. Hegel sought to reform this arbitrary procedure by introducing a strict dialectical evolution of thought. And the first step towards this was to show that the negative, distinguishing, or differentiating movement of thought is essentially related to, or rather an essential part of, its positive, constructive, or synthetic movement. On the one hand, therefore, he points out that in the negative movement of thought, by which the finite consciousness is shown to be in itself contradictory and suicidal, there is already involved a positive apprehension of that which is beyond the finite; for, as the negative is a definite negative, it includes that which is denied and something more,—and this something more is already, or at least implicitly involves, the idea that solves the contradiction. On the other hand, and for the same reason, the positive idea—the idea of the infinite which is reached by negation of the finite—cannot be taken as merely affirmative or positive; it contains in itself an essential reference to the finite by negation of which it was reached. We must not, therefore, treat it like Spinoza, as a mere *terminus ad quem*—a lion's den, in which all the tracks of thought terminate, while none are seen to emerge from it. The infinite would have no meaning for us, it would be a thought without reality, if it were not itself the finite seen *sub specie æternitatis*. The mystic intuition of "all things in God" is a dream, unless it can unfold its concentrated white light into new views of the many forms of nature and human life, with all the varied and definite hues and shapes. "*Am farbigen Abglanz haben wir das Leben.*" A theory of the world as spiritual must face or overcome the opposition of spirit and nature; it must not simply escape from the contradiction of life into the "pure ether" of thought, but must go down into the contradiction and explain it. It must, indeed, conceive the world as a unity, but it must reach this unity by a patient exhaustion of those differences and oppositions which seem to make unity absurd and impossible. Hence the negative dialectic of scepticism will find full play, not merely before philosophy as an introduction, but within it as the means of its evolution.

Connected with this, finally, is Hegel's more definite assertion, which, as we have seen, was already made in the last number of the 'Critical Journal,' that the unity to which all things must be brought is not some middle term between nature and spirit—some identity in which that, like all other distinctions, is lost; but that it is the unity of spirit with itself, as subordinating and including in itself that very nature which seems its absolute opposite. Only by this idea can we reconcile the freedom of man—in the sense that what determines him is his own

Breach with Schelling.

nature, and that alone—with his relations to that which is not himself, to the external world, and to other rational beings. The life of spirit and nature is indeed ultimately one; "the infinite expansion of nature, and absolute retraction of the *ego* upon itself, are fundamentally identical; yet both being equally real, *spirit is higher than nature*. For though in nature we have the realisation, the infinitely diversified mediation and evolution of the absolute, yet spirit, as being essentially self-conscious, when it draws back the universe into itself as it does in knowledge, at once includes in itself the outwardly expanded totality of this manifold world, and at the same time overreaches and idealises it, taking away its externality to itself and to the mind, and reflecting it all into the unity of thought."[1] In other words, nature is to be regarded not as another existence side by side with mind, but as part of its own life; for though at the lower point of view the two may appear as irreconcilable opposites, at the highest point the life of nature is seen to be but an element in the life of spirit.

The development of these different points of opposition between Hegel and Schelling is the main fact of the philosophical life of the former during the years 1803-6 —years in which Hegel continued to teach, at first as a *privat-docent*, and, after the beginning of the year 1805, as an extraordinary professor in the University of Jena. During this period Schelling was showing a continually increasing bias towards theosophy and mysticism, and some of his followers, by their exaggeration of his arbitrary methods, were bringing the philosophy of nature into discredit. All this tended to repel Hegel more and

[1] Hegel, i. 385.

more from a line of speculation which seemed to produce nothing but continual reiterations of the principle of identity, or, if it went beyond this, fell into wayward and fanciful constructions—hybrids between poetry and philosophy with the distinctive merits of neither. Accordingly, in his Jena lectures we find him insisting with even greater emphasis on the necessity of method, of clear consciousness as to the meaning and value of the categories employed in philosophy, and of a strict logical advance from step to step, so that each thought shall be evolved by distinct dialectic from that which precedes. In the same spirit he insisted, as has been before indicated, on the duty of meeting the ordinary consciousness on its own ground, and of showing from its own premises the necessity of advancing to the philosophical point of view: and it was to supply such an introduction to philosophy that he wrote his first important work, the 'Phænomenology of Spirit.' In this book Hegel gives us a kind of genetic psychology or philosophical 'Pilgrim's Progress,' in which the individual, beginning with the lowest sensuous consciousness which is possible to a rational being, is gradually led upwards, by the dialectic of his own thought, to the highest speculative idea of the world as an organic system, whose principle of unity lies in the self-conscious intelligence. The preface to the 'Phænomenology' is specially important as a landmark in the development of Hegel, because it is in it that he first decisively breaks with the school and method—or rather want of method—of Schelling, whom, however, he never names. Indeed it is, perhaps, not so much Schelling himself who is aimed at, as the general tendency—of which he was the least guilty though the most prominent representative,—the tendency, viz., to make intellectual intuition or immediate feeling, even when conceived as the gift of certain privileged natures, the organ of philosophy. In opposition to this tendency, Hegel points out the need for mediation or logical development of thought, both to bring men to the true principle of philosophy, and to develop it to a system. In reference to the former, he contends, in language which has already been quoted, that no one has a right to speak as if he had a vision of truth of which other men were incapable, since philosophy must prove its claims by meeting every one on his own ground. In reference to the latter, he argues that no one can be said really to possess a principle unless he can develop it to its consequences. "The principle of philosophy, even if it be truly apprehended, is turned to falsehood if it is taken *only* as a principle." "Everything depends upon the absolute truth being apprehended, *not merely as substance but as subject*"—*i.e.*, not as a Spinozistic identity, in which all difference is lost, but as a spiritual principle. But as such a principle it can be apprehended, only if it is seen to manifest itself in and to transcend all differences, and especially the difference of subject and object, man and nature— only, in short, if it is recognised as the principle of a system. For apart from such evolution to a system, the mere name of spirit or subject cannot mean much more than substance. Schelling's *undeveloped* spiritualism, just because it is undeveloped, is little more than Spinozism.

The 'Phænomenology' is, in a literary point of view, the most perfect of Hegel's works. It wants, indeed, the clearness, the dialectical precision, and the just proportion of parts which we find in some of his later writings; but it compensates for this by a certain imaginative richness and power of utterance, a certain fervid fluency, as of a thought which, after long brooding, had at last burst into expression. The peculiar merit of the book is not merely that its dialectical process is assisted in its expression by imagination, but that the process itself seems to become poetical and imaginative through its success in overcoming the abstractions and reconciling the oppositions with which it deals. It is not poetical philosophy; it is philosophy in its last synthesis showing itself to be poetry, thought taking fire by the rapidity and intensity of its own movement. Hegel called it his "voyage of discovery;" and it is indeed a sort of philosopher's autobiography, in which all the main forces that influenced his own development are clearly indicated. It contains the system in its first conception, when it had not yet been thoroughly objectified, or when the philosopher had not yet attempted to ascertain his own "personal equation," and allow for it: but, for that very reason, it has a special value for every one who wishes to study the genesis of the system.

CHAPTER IV.

HEGEL AFTER THE BATTLE OF JENA—THE SCHOOL AT NÜRNBERG.

HEGEL was rudely awakened from the philosophical ecstasy, as we might call it, that breathes through the last chapter of the 'Phænomenology,' by the "thunders of Jena." Ever since her first effort to quell the infant giant of the Revolution in the French war of 1794-95, Prussia, in spite of her great military force, had withdrawn from the conflict, and secured her own tranquillity amid the disasters of Germany by a somewhat narrow policy of reserve. She had held aloof from all the struggles of Austria, and had even condescended to receive rewards of territory from Napoleon for her steady subservience. She had fallen, as one of her statesmen said, into "that lowest of degradations, to steal at another man's bidding." Meanwhile under her wing the little state of Weimar had escaped the disasters of war, and its university of Jena, with its apostolical succession of Reinhold, Fichte, Schelling, and Hegel, had been the centre of the philosophic movement, as Weimar itself, with Goethe and Schiller, was the literary centre of Germany. At last, in 1806, Prussia began to see that she was destined by the conqueror to receive the reward of the Cyclops to Ulysses—to be "eaten last;" and she gathered herself together for a struggle with Napoleon, only to find her army broken to pieces and her kingdom dismembered in a campaign of a few days.

Just before the decisive battle of Jena, the French soldiers broke into the town and began to plunder. Several of them entered Hegel's lodging, and it is recorded that he met their threats by an appeal to one of their number on whose breast he noticed the ribbon of the Legion of Honour, saying that from a man with such a badge, he had a right to expect honourable treatment for a simple man of letters. As things got worse, and fire spread among the houses, Hegel put the last pages of the 'Phænomenology' in his pocket, left the rest of his property to its fate, and took refuge in the house of the Pro-rector Gabler, which was protected by the presence of a French officer of high rank. After the battle Napoleon had the fires stopped, and Hegel returned to his lodging, in which he found everything in confusion. A few days before, he had written to his friend Niethammer,—" I saw the Emperor, that world-soul, riding through the city to reconnoitre. It is in truth a strange feeling to see such an individual before one, who here, from one point, as he rides on his horse, is reaching over the world, and remoulding it. For the Prussians one could not prognosticate anything better; but in the space between Thursday and Monday, such advances have been made as are possible only for this extraordinary man. . . . As I let you know before, all now wish good fortune to the French army, which

Political Opinions. 67

cannot fail in the immense difference between its leaders and soldiers, and those of its enemies."

A word of commentary seems necessary to explain this last utterance. Hegel was not, like Goethe, devoid of German patriotism. He had already written two pamphlets — which the rapid progress of events had prevented him from publishing — in which he endeavoured to trace the causes of the political and military weakness of Germany, and also to point out how the empire, and the minor States included in it, might be regenerated. But as a Southern, he looked to Austria, the inheritor of the imperial tradition, as the centre of resistance, rather than to Prussia, which at this time he regarded as a lifeless machine of bureaucracy. No more than any one else could he anticipate how in a few years the reforms of Stein and Scharnhorst and Hardenberg were to renew the energies of the kingdom of Frederic the Great, and to make it the protagonist of Germany in the war of liberation. Hence he seems to have had no other feeling about the immediate contest than contempt for Prussia and admiration for Napoleon, who, as he said at a later time, "put the greatest genius into military victory only to show how little, after all, mere victory counts for." But that he did not, even at this time, despair of the ultimate result for Germany, is shown by a letter of his addressed to an old pupil called Zellmann, who had written to him in a despairing way about the future. In this letter he tells Zellmann to look beyond the immediate failure to its causes, and to see in them the promise of recovery. "Science," he declares, "is the only theodicy; it alone can keep us from taking events with the stupid astonishment of an animal, or, with short-sighted cleverness, ascribing them to the accidents of the moment or of the talents of an individual, and supposing that the fate of empires depends on a hill being or not being occupied by soldiery,—as well as from lamenting over them, as at the victory of injustice and the defeat of justice. The French nation, by the bath of its revolution, has been freed from many institutions which the spirit of man has left behind like its baby shoes, and which therefore weighed upon it, as they still weigh upon others, as lifeless fetters. What, however, is more, the individuals of that nation have, in the shock of revolution, cast off the fear of death and the life of custom, which in the change of scene has now ceased to have any meaning in itself. It is this that gives them the prevailing force which they are showing against other nations. Hence especially comes their preponderance over the cloudy and undeveloped spirit of the Germans, who, however, if they are once forced to cast off their inertia, will rouse themselves to action, and *preserving in their contact with outward things the intensity of their inner life, will perchance surpass their teachers.*" [1]

In the meantime, while he was expressing this lofty confidence in the justice of destiny, Hegel's own fortunes were reduced to the lowest ebb. The war, which destroyed the university life of Jena, had left him so absolutely destitute, that we find Goethe commissioning his friend Knebel to lend him a few dollars for his immediate necessities. In these circumstances, he was glad to accept the work, which his friend Niethammer procured for him, of editing a newspaper at Bamberg. A German

[1] Hegel, xvii. 628.

newspaper in those times could only be a bare record of events, without any comment or criticism whatever. No independent leading articles were permitted under the rule of Napoleon. And Hegel, while he is said to have done his editorial work, such as it was, in an efficient and workmanlike manner, seems to have regarded it merely as a temporary means of keeping the wolf from the door. In a letter to Knebel, he takes a somewhat humorous view of his own position; tells him that the smallest contributions of news from his part of the country will be thankfully received; and adds, "I have made my guiding-star the Biblical saying, the truth of which I have learnt by experience,—'Seek ye first food and clothing, and the kingdom of heaven shall be added unto you.'"

After a year of this work, Niethammer, who had become what we may call the head of the educational department for the Protestant part of Bavaria, got Hegel recommended to the somewhat more congenial occupation of Rector in the Gymnasium at Nürnberg. Bavaria was one of the smaller States of Germany which Napoleon treated with special favour, and which he aggrandised by accessions of territory, in order to make use of them as checks and rivals of the greater German powers of Austria and Prussia. What they lost by this anti-patriotic position was, however, partly compensated by their contact with the reforming spirit of France, which enabled them more rapidly to rid themselves of the semi-feudal relics of the old imperial system. In Bavaria especially, the new ideas of organisation and enlightenment inspired the policy of the Government, which about this time had drawn into its employment not only Hegel and Niethammer, but also Schelling, Paulus, Schubert, and others of the best talents of Germany. Niethammer, Hegel's patron, was zealous for the reform of the old system of education, which he sought to revive mainly by the aid of a less mechanical study of classical antiquity, but also by the introduction into the teaching of the schools of at least the elements of the new philosophy. Hegel willingly, and with his whole heart, made himself the instrument of this movement, so far at least as the first part of the scheme was concerned; for to him the classics were for general culture—what Spinoza was for philosophy—the "spiritual bath" through which the mind was to be freed from the narrowness of its merely natural sympathies, and prepared for a wider and freer culture. In this spirit he spoke in one of his addresses to his school at the end of the academical year. "For some centuries," he declares, "this is the ground upon which all culture has stood, out of which it has sprung, with which it has been in constant connection. As the natural organisms —plants and animals—withdraw themselves from the immediate influence of gravity, but yet cannot leave behind them this element of their being, so all art and science has developed from this basis, and though it has become independent in itself, yet has it not freed itself from the memory of that more ancient culture. As Antæus renewed his forces by touching his mother earth, so science and culture, in every revival of their energy, have raised themselves to light out of a return to antiquity." Hegel then goes on to condemn the old system of teaching Latin to the exclusion of all other things, and especially of the mother tongue, "for a nation cannot be regarded as cultured which does not possess the treasures of science in its own speech." Nevertheless, while the ancient tongues must be kept in their proper place, they remain the essential basis of everything,—" the spiritual bath, the profane baptism which gives to the soul the first indelible tone and tincture for truth and science." " If the first paradise was the paradise of human *nature*, this is the second, the higher paradise of the human *spirit*, which, in its fair naturalness, freedom, depth, and brightness, here comes forth like a bride out of her chamber. The first wild majesty of the rise of spiritual life in the East is in classical literature circumscribed by the dignity of form, and softened into beauty; its depth shows itself no longer in confusion, obscurity, and inflation, but lies open before us in simple clearness; its brightness is not a childish play, but covers a sadness that knows the hardness of fate, yet is not by it driven out of freedom and measure. I do not think I am asserting too much when I say, that he who has not known the works of the ancients, has lived without knowing beauty."[1]

The introduction of philosophy into the schools Hegel did not much approve; but he conformed to the direction of his superiors, and even drew up a kind of Propædeutic to Philosophy, which has since been published, and which, with all the rector's explanation, must have greatly puzzled the clever boys of Nürnberg. He encouraged his pupils to question and even to interrupt him, and often spent the whole hour of instruction in meeting the difficulties which they suggested. It requires, as some one has said, a great mastery over a

[1] Hegel, xvi. 139.

science to teach its rudiments well; and Hegel afterwards recognised that the effort to express himself with the necessary simplicity and definiteness, to free his ideas from all obscurities of subjective association, and so to bring them into relation with untrained minds, was of great service to himself, both in increasing his effectiveness as a speaker, and in enabling him to give a more strictly scientific expression to his system than it had already received in the 'Phænomenology.' As a schoolmaster, he seems to have been thoroughly successful—showing in the general management of the affairs of the school the same practical talent which he had proved in the editorship of his newspaper, and at the same time gaining the respect and confidence of his pupils by the impression of moral and intellectual weight which he carried with him. He was a strict disciplinarian, and altogether opposed to the Pestalozzian ideas of education then in vogue, according to which the teaching must accommodate itself to the individuality of the pupil, and as little as possible exercise any pressure upon his natural tendencies. The basis of sound education was, for Hegel, obedience and self-surrender—the submission of the mind to an external lesson, which must be learnt by every one, and even learnt by rote, with utter disregard of individual tastes and desires; only out of this self-abnegation, and submission to be guided and taught, could any originality spring that was worth preserving. Yet, in insisting upon strict order and method, Hegel seems to have avoided the extreme of petty interference, and to have tolerated the frolic and licence of his schoolboys, even beyond the point which is now considered desirable. One of his Nürnberg pupils gives the following somewhat characteristic anecdote : " I remember that in 1812 a dancing-master came to Nürnberg, and, with Hegel's permission, opened a course of lessons at the gymnasium, for which the members were requested to put down their names. Naturally almost every one subscribed. After a time, however, some of us became discontented. The dancing-master, skilful enough in his art, was, as is not unusual, a coxcomb; the wearisome exercises in mannerly deportment, the standing in stocks to turn the toes outwards, &c., were not liked. . . . In short, some of the scholars planned how to withdraw from their engagement. But that was impossible without Hegel's consent, and I and another were sent to lay our grievances before him. But what a reception we got! I scarcely know how we got down the stairs. He would not see the dancing-master lose the fees guaranteed to him; and, in short, we were obliged to dance, stand in stocks, and make our salutations till the end of the summer."

On September 16, 1811, Hegel was married to Marie von Tucher, a lady of an old Nürnberg family. She was, we are told, a woman of gentle, aristocratic manners, of fine feminine impulsiveness and feminine belief in impulse; a friend of Jean Paul, and strongly interested in the fine arts, as we may gather from the contents of her husband's letters to her. In many ways she was the "opposite counterpart" of the reserved strength, the deep-searching systematic reflection, and the *bourgeois* simplicity and even plainness of her husband, who never entirely lost a tinge of provincialism in his manners and speech. During the courtship Hegel addressed to her some verses, which are rather better than those he usually wrote, but which have too much philosophic analysis of love to be quite good poetic expressions of it. The German open-heartedness in these matters allows us to see something of the slight jars which were naturally produced at first between people of such opposite characters and tendencies as they came to know each other more intimately after the engagement. Hegel has to explain his ruthless masculine way of denouncing certain tendencies and views with which his Marie feels some sympathy. "In respect to myself, and the way in which I express my views, I confess that when I have to condemn principles, I too easily lose sight of the way and manner in which they are present in a particular individual—in this case, in you—and that I am apt to take them too earnestly because I see them in their universal bearing and consequence, which you do not think of,—which, indeed, for you, are not in them at all. Yet *you* know well, that although character and principles of judgment are not the same thing, yet that it is not indifferent to character what principles of judgment are adopted: and *I*, on my side, know equally well that principles of judgment, when they contradict the character, are even of less import with your sex than with ours. . . . There are men who torment their wives in order to gain, from their bearing under provocation, a new consciousness of their love and patience. I do not think that I am so perverse; but I can hardly repent that I have pained you, so much has the strength and inwardness of my love been confirmed by the deeper insight into your nature which I have gained." The marriage was in all ways a happy one, and Hegel could now face the world with a heart at rest. "When a man has got work which suits him, and a wife whom he loves," he writes to his friend Niethammer, "he may be said to have made up his accounts with life." Two sons were born of this marriage, Karl and Immanuel—the former of whom is now a Professor of History at Erlangen. Hegel never had a large income, even at the height of his fame, and his household was arranged with orderly frugality: except in emergencies, he never had more than one maid-servant. But he found money to make his household life tasteful, and to provide for domestic indulgences and surprises. His favourite recreation was in making short excursions with his family. During the Nürnberg period, he had also the happiness of having with him for a time his sister Christiane, to whom he was much attached.

During the quiet years at Nürnberg which followed his marriage, 1812-16, Hegel produced what is his greatest work in a purely scientific point of view, the 'Logic,' —with all its defects, the one work which the modern world has to put beside the 'Metaphysic' of Aristotle. In it the fundamental idea of his system—that the unity to which all things must be referred is a spiritual or self-conscious principle — is fully developed, and proved in the only way in which such proof is possible, —by showing that every other category or principle which might explain the world, is ultimately resolvable, or rather by its own dialectical movement resolves itself, into this. Thus "Being," "Measure," "Essence," "Force," "Law," "Substance," "Cause,"—whatever names have been given to the identity that underlies all differences,—are shown to be expressions of a thought which, when it is made explicit, is found to mean or involve the principle of self-consciousness. When this is proved, therefore, the further work of philosophy must be simply to apply this key to the concrete forms of nature and history, and to show how, by its means, they are to be made intelligible. This, however, will be more fully explained in the sequel.

Hegel, however, had not in the gymnasium quite the work that suited him, and frequently during those eight years he had been making inquiries as to different university appointments, in which he would be freed from the practical cares of a school, and find a fit audience for the best of his thoughts. Meanwhile his fame was gradually rising, and bringing him into relations with many philosophical writers and students, who were reaching with undefined aims beyond the philosophies of Fichte and Schelling, and who welcomed the new light of the 'Phænomenology' and the 'Logic.' All at once, in July 1816, when he was just on the point of issuing the last volume of the 'Logic,' he received three offers of chairs of philosophy from Erlangen, Heidelberg, and Berlin—though in the invitation from Berlin a certain doubt was expressed whether his long cessation from university work had not deprived him of the power of effective speech necessary in a university. Hegel accepted the invitation to Heidelberg, and at last, in his forty-seventh year, attained that position of freedom from other cares, and of direct influence over the university teaching of philosophy, which he had so long desired.

CHAPTER V.

HEGEL AS A PROFESSOR AT HEIDELBERG AND BERLIN— HIS CHARACTER AND INFLUENCE.

DURING the eight years which Hegel spent in the Nürnberg Gymnasium, the fortunes of Germany had undergone a great change. The disasters of the Russian campaign had given the first shock to the seemingly unconquerable power of the French Emperor, and Prussia, regenerated by the silent reforms of Stein and Hardenberg, had commenced the German insurrection, which ended in the overthrow of Napoleon. The Congress of Vienna had done what it could to evoke some kind of order out of the confused result of war, and also it had sought in some degree to bridle the national spirit which the war had called forth. But Germany was still agitated like the sea after a storm. The undefined expectation of some great result from so many sacrifices, the effort of the representatives of the old Germanic system to reassert those historical rights which had disappeared, the necessity of giving some satisfaction to the desire of national unity, and the policy of the different dynasties leading them to reassert their separate independence,—all these tendencies and influences were confusedly struggling with each other. On the whole, the desire of peace and rest after so many troublous years, and the fear of revolution produced by the example of France, prevailed over all other feelings. The German nation had no clear idea of what it wanted, and was not willing to rouse itself to any continued efforts to remould its institutions. All that could be expected was that some working compromise should be secured, out of which better things might grow, as the times became ripe for a new movement of progress.

Hegel was deeply interested, as we shall see, in the political problem, but his first natural feeling was that the time had come when the interests of culture and philosophy, which had been silenced by the noise of battle, might find a hearing; and this is the idea expressed in his introductory address at Heidelberg. "While the spirit of the world was so much occupied with real interests, it could not turn inwards, or gather itself together in itself: but now that the stream of events, on which we were carried along so rapidly, has been checked—now that the German nation has redeemed itself by the sword from the worst of tyrannies, and regained its nationality, that foundation of all higher life—we may hope that besides the kingdom of this world, on which all thoughts and efforts have been hitherto concentrated, the kingdom of God may also be thought of; in other words, that besides political and other worldly interests, science and philosophy, the free interests of intelligence, may also rise to newness of life." This hope is the more reasonable, Hegel declares, as philosophy is the peculiar vocation of the

German nation. "History shows us that even when all but the name of philosophy was lost in other lands, it has maintained itself as the peculiar possession of the German nation. We have received from nature the high calling to be guardians of this sacred fire, as in earlier times the world-spirit maintained the highest consciousness in the Jewish nation, that from them it might rise again as a new spiritual force in the world. . . . Let us greet together the dawn of a better time, when the spirit, that has hitherto been driven out of itself, may return to itself again, and win room and space wherein to found a kingdom of its own."

Hegel began to lecture with an audience of four, which, however, gradually increased to twenty for one of his courses and thirty for the other. Heidelberg afforded him opportunities of extending his knowledge of art, and it was there that he first lectured on Æsthetic. The work, however, which mainly engaged him was his Encyclopædia, a general outline of his system, consisting of short compressed paragraphs, which he often made the basis of his lectures. This work was afterwards much extended and developed, but in its first form it has a compactness, a brief energy and conclusiveness of expression, which he never surpassed. He is described as at this time rather withdrawing from general society, and so intensely concentrated on the effort of applying his principles to nature and history, as sometimes to lose all sense of outward things. His students thought him idle, because they used to see him standing for hours at his window, looking out on the misty hills and woods of Heidelberg; and it is related that on one occasion, as he was walking to the university, after a heavy rain, he left a shoe in the mud without being conscious of the loss. On the general body of the students his influence was not great, but he gradually drew to himself those who had any aptitude for philosophy. And during his whole stay in Heidelberg his name was steadily rising, in spite of the general tendencies of the place, which seem to have been rather unfavourable to philosophic studies.

Hegel wrote at this time two rather important papers in the 'Heidelberg Jahrbücher,'—one on Jacobi, and the other on the constitutional struggles of Würtemberg,— papers which first defined Hegel's attitude to the religious and political life of his time. Jacobi, like Fichte, had been vigorously attacked by Hegel in the 'Critical Journal,' when he and Schelling were fighting their early battle against the philosophical world; but now greater clearness had brought greater calm, and Hegel recognised that in aim, if not in method, he was at one with Jacobi. The arbitrary intuitional ways of the latter, whose ideas were generally put forth like mere "shots from a pistol," his want of dialectic, and his inability to recognise his own ideas when they were presented to him in other language, Hegel still criticises. But he recognises that, after all, Jacobi's intuitions were right, and that, in his own way, he had kept alive the essential idea of philosophy—the idea that the principle of all things is spiritual. This *amende honorable* much comforted the old man, who of late had received somewhat rough usage from Schelling, and who now came to Heidelberg to embrace Hegel and thank him for his acknowledgment.

In the second paper, on the proceedings of the Estates

The Idea of the State.

of Würtemberg, we have Hegel's first *published* utterance on politics, though, as we have seen, he had all along taken a deep interest in the political movement, and had twice before been on the point of giving his views to the world. The changes through which his opinions on this subject passed went on *pari passu* with the general development of his system. The youthful enthusiasm for liberty kindled in him by the French Revolution, was changed by the experiences of the time and his own advance beyond individualistic views of society, into a conception of the state as an organic unity, in which the individual should find at once the means of his education as a moral and rational being, and the sphere for the exercise of his special gifts. In the time of Hegel's closest alliance with Schelling, his conception of the unity of the state was so strict that it even approximated to a revival of the Greek aristocratic socialism. Even then, however, he was conscious that the Greek ideal could not be applied without modification to modern life; and that the modern state must seek to combine the unity of the ancient republic with an acknowledgment of the independent rights and personal freedom of the individual, which to the ancient republican, to Plato and Aristotle, would have seemed anarchy. The modern state must not be an extended family or socialistic community in which the individual is lost; nor, on the other hand, must it be a mere "social contract" of individuals who have no vital relations to each other—no relations which are not produced by their own will. Yet in some sense it must embrace both these ideas, and reconcile them in one. Like a family, it must be based on nature, on a community of race and language; it must rest on relations that are, and are acknowledged to be, independent of all the mere caprice of individuals. This end, as Hegel thought, could be best attained in a hereditary monarchy, where the person of the monarch becomes as it were the fixed point which is raised above all discussion, the representative of the historical unity of the nation. On the other hand, the state must also be a "civic society," in which individuals are secured in their private rights of person and property, and allowed every opportunity of pursuing their particular aims and developing their special abilities in competition and co-operation with each other. And in order that natural unity and social freedom may be combined, the monarch must be a constitutional monarch, ruling through his ministers, who are in contact with and responsible to the Parliament, and the people must be organised in communities and corporations, from which again representatives to the Parliament shall be chosen. In this way the Government will be at once permanent and progressive, raised above the direct revolutionary action of the many—a real leader of the people, and yet continually receiving new support and development from the constitutionally expressed will of the nation. Hegel, it will be observed, does not think of a constitutional monarchy as a slightly veiled democracy, at least according to Rousseau's idea of democracy as a Government which only collects and records the decisions of its subjects; he thinks of it as—what indeed every real Government must be, whatever its name—a guiding and directing power. Nor is this irreconcilable with the fact that no Government can be powerful that does not express the will of the people,—for, as Hegel says, "the people never knows what it wills." It is the business of Government at once to make it conscious of its will, and to carry it into effect. It may be questioned whether Hegel was right in supposing that a hereditary monarchy is necessary, or will in the end prove to be even the best expedient, to secure this result. But, in any case, there were good grounds for believing that was so under the actual conditions of the time in England and in Prussia. Hegel's ideal seems, indeed, to have lain midway between the English and the Prussian systems,—having more of democracy than the latter, and implying more of direct initiative on the part of the Government than the former, as might be expected in the political system of one who had witnessed the great reforms of Stein and Hardenberg.

This ideal of the state was, in its main points at least, already developed by Hegel before he left Jena; for it is implied, if not directly expressed, in his unpublished pamphlet on the imperial system. This pamphlet appears from internal evidence to have been written shortly after the Treaty of Luneville, when the imperial system had already shown its weakness for the defence of Germany against the French. It begins with the words, "Germany is no longer a state, but, as a French writer has said, a constituted anarchy." This it has learnt by experience in war; for "war is the touchstone which proves whether there is a real coherence in the different parts of the state, and whether they are prepared to make any sacrifices for it." Hegel therefore calls on his countrymen not to waste their time in vain complaints of their fate, but to try to understand it, and to see in it not the working of caprice and accident, but the necessary result of the political paralysis into which Germany had fallen. The "Holy Roman Empire" had gradually sunk under the abuses of the feudal system, according to which each part of the whole political body was so strongly intrenched in its particular rights, that the general power of the state was annihilated. An imperial army was a theme for jest, for every contributor tried to contribute as little as possible; imperial justice was a mockery, for a suit in the courts of the empire never came to an end. An endless formalism, which in its tenderness for particular rights never allowed any right to be realised, might console itself with the maxim, *Fiat justitia pereat mundus;* but it was time to consider whether that could be really justice which made Germany perish. This system, whose weakness had long been hidden under the *magni nominis umbra* of the empire, was stripped of its disguise by the calamities of the times. "Only the memory of the former bond preserves yet a semblance of union, as fallen fruits may be known to have belonged to the tree because they lie beneath it, though its shadow neither protects them from corruption nor from the power of the elements to which they now belong."

Hegel therefore calls for a renewal of the imperial authority, which shall not, indeed, imitate the centralisation of France, but which, while admitting the self-government or "home rule" of the separate provinces in matters that concern themselves, shall yet bring them together in a real effective political union under one monarch and one government. "The greatness of modern states makes it impossible to realise the ancient idea of the personal participation of every freeman in the general government. Both for execution and deliberation, the power of the state must gather to a centre. But if this centre is maintained in independence by the reverence of the people, and consecrated in its unchangeableness in the person of a monarch, determined by the natural law of birth, the Government may, without fear or jealousy, leave the subordinate systems and corporations to determine in their own way most of the relations which arise in society, and every rank, city, commune, &c., to enjoy the freedom of doing that which lies within its sphere." Hegel's ideal is therefore not that of a machine moved by one spring, which communicates motion to all the rest of the endlessly complicated works, but of a social organism in which life is continually streaming from the centre to the extremities, and back again from them to the centre; and he points out that, while a centralised despotic government has nothing to calculate on beyond its definite known resources, a free state has besides, in every part of it, points of force from which new resources may spring.

Hegel, however, felt that such a revolution as he contemplated, by which the old structure of privilege should be turned into an organic state, was one of those things which do not come of themselves, but that there was need of force to suppress the opposition of the different provinces which were so strongly intrenched in their particular rights. And in words that are somewhat prophetic,—though the prophecy was long of accomplishment,—he calls for a hero, to realise by "blood and iron" the political regeneration of Germany. "Though all parts would gain by Germany becoming one state, and though public opinion has been so far educated that the need of it is deeply and definitely felt, yet such an event is never the fruit of deliberation, but always of force. The common mass of the German nation with their provincial estates, which know of nothing but the division of the separate sections of their race, and look upon their union as something altogether strange and monstrous, must be gathered into one by the violence of a conqueror; they must be compelled by him to regard themselves as belonging to one Germany. Such a Theseus must have magnanimity enough to grant to the nation which he has formed out of scattered peoples a share in that which is the common interest; he must have character enough, if not to submit to be rewarded with ingratitude, like Theseus, yet to be willing to brave, by reason of the direction of government which he keeps in his own hands, the hate which Richelieu and other great men have brought upon themselves, when they crushed all particular wills and factious interests to secure the general good."

The rapid advance of events, the succession of blows by which Napoleon annihilated the German empire, apparently outstripped Hegel's pen, and this pamphlet was never completed. Nor, in spite of the great outburst of German patriotism in the war of liberation and the hopes which it produced, would the Congress of Vienna listen to the idea of a revival of the empire. Hence, after the war, Germany resolved itself into a very loose confederation of states, each of which was left to develop in its own way, only with the understanding that "Estates" or a Parliament were to be introduced by every Government for its own subjects.

Swabian Politics.

One of the first states to enter upon the path of reform was Würtemberg, the territory of which had been doubled by the Napoleonic policy. The king, one of the most arbitrary and tyrannical of princes, but a man of statesmanlike ability, anticipated the attack on his despotism by offering to his people a charter, in which provision was made for their representation in a parliament, and also, with some reserves, for parliamentary control over the legislation and taxation of the kingdom, but in which, at the same time, the privileges of the nobles, as well as the special rights and monopolies guaranteed to certain other classes in the old semi-feudal constitution of Würtemberg, were abolished. Suspicion of the king's motives, however, and a somewhat reactionary patriotism, united the people with the Estates in their rejection of the royal offer, and in their demand for the restoration of the "good old laws." The death of the king and the accession of a popular heir, who had been one of the heroes of the war of liberation, did not put an end to this strange struggle between a despotic Government seeking to force the people to be free, and a people supporting the abuses and monopolies of feudalism. But the sympathy of Germany, which at first had been with the resistance of the Estates, soon began to change sides, and even in Würtemberg—at least in those parts of it which did not belong to the old duchy—a party in favour of the king's proposals was forming itself. It was at this time that Hegel, moved thereto, it is said, by the request of the minister Von Vangenheim, struck into the battle. Filled as he was with a sense of the evils which the "good old laws" had brought upon Germany, he could not but take the side of the king; and nowhere do we find a more thorough and merciless exposure of the defects of the semi-feudal arrangements pertaining to the imperial system, than in the paper which he wrote on the subject. Hegel, however, in his vigorous polemic, shows himself more of a partisan than we should have expected, and does not give us any glimpses of the reasons which partly excused the wrong-headedness and obstinacy of his Swabian fellow-countrymen. Indeed it has to be allowed generally, that in controversy Hegel, if not unfair, is at least ruthless. There is no malice, nor, I think, *personal* bitterness in his polemic; but it is unsparing, unsympathetic, and gathers itself into weighty words of irony and indignation which were felt like blows, and sometimes roused violent opposition and anger against him. We are often reminded of his own admission to his wife, that in assailing principles which seemed to him wrong, he forgot to allow for "the manner and way in which they are present in particular individuals." And it was only to be expected, when he treated thus persons as representatives of ideas, that, on the other hand, words which were really directed by him against ideas should be interpreted as personal attacks.

The complete expression of Hegel's political theories in his 'Philosophy of Right' was not published till a later date, when he had been transferred to Berlin, which was beginning to be recognised as the scientific as well as the political centre of Germany. By the thorough reforms carried out in the hour of her apparent ruin, by the reorganisation of her army and the foundation of Berlin University, and by her energy and sacrifices in the war of liberation, Prussia had gained, and, as it turned out, permanently gained, the leadership of Germany. And though Austria was now seeking, with some success, to withdraw her from her political task, and to entangle her in a reactionary and repressive policy, yet even at the worst, the process of internal improvement was never entirely checked, and the alliance which she had formed with science and philosophy was never entirely broken. In 1816, Hegel had already drawn the attention of Solger, Niebuhr, and other men of influence in Berlin, as the one man who could fill with credit the vacant chair of Fichte, and in 1818 the proposal was renewed and accepted.

From this time until his death in 1831, Hegel held a commanding position as the greatest teacher of philosophy in the most important university of Germany. He was now in his forty-ninth year, fully possessed of himself, strong in the consciousness of the truth which he had grasped, and of the method by which he had developed it. The long delay of recognition, if it had taken away something of the first poetic vividness of conception and expression, had brought clearness, definiteness, and proportion to his treatment of the different parts and aspects of knowledge, and had enabled him to work out his principles to a system. On the other hand, it had inevitably given to his mind a certain rigidity, a certain incompliant firmness and disinclination to compromise, which was apt to be felt as tyrannical by those who were not in complete sympathy with him. The long solitary work of construction, in which he had had to be sufficient for himself, had taken away from him the capacity to give and take which belongs to youth. Nor were his eight years' labour as a schoolmaster probably without influence on his character. "I am a schoolmaster," he once said, "who has to teach philosophy, and, perhaps partly for that reason, am possessed with the idea that philosophy, as truly as geometry, must be a regular structure of ideas which is capable of being taught." "His main influence upon the Berliners," says his biographer, "was that he formally put them to school, and with *naïve* inflexibleness made them learn his system." Though in a sense his philosophy was rooted in the idea of freedom, it was also penetrated with the consciousness that real freedom is possible only through discipline; and even the Prussian tendency to introduce into everything a kind of military drill was not unwelcome to him. As Socrates was compared to those figures of Silenus which contained within the image of an Olympic god, so it may be said that in Hegel we find an idealist, for whom truth is poetry and religion one with philosophy, in the dress of a punctual and orderly civil servant of the Prussian Government.

The great danger of a position such as Hegel now held,—in close alliance with the Government, employed by it in testing the candidates for the scholastic profession, and often consulted by it in reference to academical appointments,—was that it tended too much to confuse the official and the philosopher, and to cast a suspicion of political reserve and accommodation upon all the conservative, or apparently conservative, tendencies of his social and religious speculation. Starting with the revolutionary principle, Hegel, by the natural development of his thought, had, as we have seen, been led to a view of things which was neither revolutionary nor reactionary, because based upon the idea of the evolution of humanity as an organism. He had learned to recognise that "the real is the rational," that the "soul of the world is just;" yet not in the sense of a mere glorification of the *status quo*, but in the sense that history is the progressive manifestation of reason, and that, therefore, no true reform is possible which is not in its essence a development—*i.e.*, which is not already contained in germ in that which has to be reformed. It is vain to command the seed to become an oak unless it is an acorn. Mere abstract ideals, therefore, are worthless, and their application can only lead to a general overturn without reconstruction. The revolutionary contempt of the past is fatal to all real progress, for it is only in the past that we can find such an explanation of the present as may enable us to see in it the germ of the future,—"the spirit of the years to come, yearning to mix itself with life." In religion, also, Hegel had gradually outgrown the bare negations of the *Aufklärung*, and the Hellenism of his youth, and had learnt to recognise, in the Christian idea of self-realisation through self-sacrifice, the principle that explains the intellectual and moral life of man and the nature of the universe in which he lives. Such a view separated him at once from the Revolution and the reaction, from the prevailing rationalism and from the reviving orthodoxy; and it was certain to be misunderstood by the partisans of both. Especially was it natural that to liberals in theology and politics Hegel should seem to be an obscurantist and a political quietist,—an "official philosopher," won by the bribes of place and power to maintain the cause of obstruction with the weapons of reason. Nor can it be said that Hegel took much pains to avoid such misconception. His denunciation of the revolutionary sophisms, and especially of the sentimental politics of Fries, whom in the preface to the 'Philosophy of Right' he calls the "ringleader of the hosts of shallowness," seemed to be no fair philosophical controversy at a time when the Government, in the panic that followed the murder of Kotzebue, were adopting strict measures of repression in the universities, and Fries himself was in danger of being driven from his chair. When, however, a writer in the 'Literary Review' of Halle pointed to this coincidence, and characterised Hegel's attack as an "ignoble" persecution of a man who was down, Hegel was deeply wounded and incensed, and even made the matter worse by complaining to the minister, Altenstein, that such an insinuation should be directed against him in a Review supported by the Government. Hegel declared that he had never once thought of Fries as a private person, but only of his principles; but though this declaration might be true —though, indeed, from a consideration of his general character, we may say certainly that it *was* true—yet Hegel should have remembered that above all things it is needful for a philosopher to take care that the weapons of the spirit should not seem to be used to help the weapons of the flesh. In like manner, Hegel's approximation to orthodoxy, his desire to show that in all essentials he was one with the Christian church, and his attacks upon the ordinary rationalism, exposed him, because of his official position, to the suspicion of compromising unworthily the interests of scientific truth, especially as he did *not* dwell with the same emphasis on the great, though in the main formal, changes—and especially the complete rejection of ordinary supernaturalism—which are involved in the Hegelian interpretation of Christianity.

Yet, on the whole, Hegel's attitude is neither unnatural nor inconsistent. If he felt in some degree the influence of the Restoration period—if a certain weariness of political movement is visible in the writings of his latest years—if he shows, as time goes on, an increasing proneness to reconciling views, and a disinclination to insist on a complete sifting of terms upon which the reconciliation should be made, — we need not wonder at a change which is the ordinary result of age, and was above all natural to one who had lived through such a period of overturn and renewal. "Finally, after forty years of war and unmeasurable confusion, an old heart might rejoice to see an end of it all, and the beginning of a period of peaceful satisfaction," as he said in one of his latest lectures, in reference to the French Revolution of 1830. But Hegel knew, as he immediately goes on to show, that there were discords and unresolved antagonisms which would not let men rest in what had been attained. Apart from such "tints of the setting sun," such natural leaning to rest in the attained, there is no trace of reaction in Hegel. Nowhere do we find any unfaithfulness to his fundamental principles, or a willingness to compromise any of the results that flowed from the natural development of his thought. If he attacks the *Aufklärung*, it is under the "modern standard of the free spirit," and with a distinct rejection of the principle of authority in all its forms. If his polemic is more frequently directed against the extravagances of revolutionary theory than against the sophistry of reaction, it is not because his philosophy has any special kinship with the latter, but rather for an opposite reason—because of that necessity of development which forces every new principle into a struggle with its immediate predecessor. Hegel, in fact, assumed, perhaps prematurely, that the scepticism of the *Aufklärung* had completed its work, and that the conflict with orthodoxy and the struggle with feudality was so far settled and done with, that it was now safe to recognise the substantial unity of the life that once expressed itself in these forms with that which expressed itself in his own philosophy; while with those who stood nearer to himself, and started from the same principle of reason and liberty, he felt himself obliged to fight out the battle to the end.

Meanwhile the allies whom Hegel was willing to acknowledge were not always willing to acknowledge him. The orthodox suspected philosophy *et dona ferentem*, and refused to trust to a dialectical proof of Christian ideas, which they feared to be no proof of Christianity as they understood it. And if statesmen like Altenstein and Hardenberg, who were liberals at heart, and who promoted Hegel before the reaction had fairly set in, were willing to look with favour on his political speculations, yet, towards the end of Hegel's life, when the policy of repression was finally adopted, a suspicion seems to have arisen in the Court that there was some "perilous stuff" in the 'Philosophy of Right,'—as indeed there was for a Government which was still refusing to grant many of those popular institutions which that book declares to be necessary for a free people. Hegel's last days were disturbed by a dispute with his old pupil Gans, which is said to have arisen from the democratic inferences drawn by the latter from the 'Philosophy of Right.' And the rise, after his death, of a branch of the Hegelian school, which exaggerated to distortion those very aspects of the Hegelian theory on which the philosopher himself had seemed to lay less emphasis, was the natural reaction from its apparent temporary identification with the Prussian system of State and Church. Philosophy, like religion, must seek to view human life in relation to those principles which are at the making and the unmaking of states; it cannot "sit on a hill remote" to reason about abstractions; it cannot but attempt to comprehend that greatest of organisms, the State, which, in the "architectonic of its rationality," is the highest result of the conscious and unconscious working of reason in the life of man; but, like religion, it must suffer loss, when it is drawn down into the region of immediate practical politics, and confounded with the attack and defence of special measures and institutions.

Hegel's real work, however, had little to do with the changing politics of the Government which employed him. He was a teacher, and not a statesman,—a teacher whose main mission in life it was to find expression for one great leading idea, which should reconcile men to the world, and revive the power that seemed to be passing away from the Christian faith, as well as to imbue his pupils with the new philosophic method, by which that idea was to be developed and applied. For this work his position at Berlin gave him a great opportunity. During the first ten years of his residence his influence on the students of the great university was continually increasing; and though after that period the decline of bodily vigour, or at least of the buoyancy necessary to the successful teacher, began to be perceptible, he was, till the end of his life, in 1831, recognised as occupying in philosophy a place almost analogous to that which Goethe held in the world of letters. His pupils, indeed, were fond of associating the two names together; and the circumstance that their birthdays fell on successive days was used in the year 1826 to unite them in one continuous festival, in which the enthusiasm of Hegel's present and past students found its culminating expression. Hegel himself seemed to take this apotheosis as a proof that his work was nearly done, when, in his address to his assembled friends, he said, with that grand simplicity that always marked his acceptance of the facts of life: "If one lives long enough, one must be content to take this also among the experiences of life, no longer to see one's self beside, or at the head of, younger men, but to stand to them as age to youth; and that point of life has now come for me."

If we ask for the sources of this influence, we cannot attribute it to any of those external advantages of address and manner which distinguished Fichte and Schelling. Cousin, who may be said to have been the pupil of both Hegel and Schelling, contrasts the flowing eloquence of the latter with the "powerful, though embarrassed, diction, the fixed gaze, and the clouded brow" of Hegel, "which seemed to be an image of thought turned back upon itself." And from Hotho, one of Hegel's most distinguished pupils, we have an account of him, which—though something may be allowed for the fervour of discipleship—enables us vividly to realise the impression made by him both in public and in private.

"It was at the beginning of my student-life that one morning I ventured to present myself, shyly, yet full of trust, in Hegel's room. He sat before a broad writing-table, and was impatiently turning over the books and papers which lay heaped in some disorder upon it. His figure was bent in premature age, and yet had a look of native toughness and force; a yellow-grey dressing-gown hung from his shoulders, covering his person down to the ground. There was nothing very noticeable in his general external appearance—no imposing height or charm of manner; rather an impression of a certain honest downrightness, as of some citizen of the olden time, was conveyed in his whole bearing. The first impression of his face, however, I shall not easily forget. Pale and relaxed, his features hung down as if lifeless; no destructive passion was mirrored in them, but only a long history of patient thought. The agony of doubt, the ferment of unappeasable mental disturbance, seemed never to have tortured, never at least to have overpowered him, in all his forty years of brooding, seeking, and finding; only the restless impulse to develop the early germ of happily discovered truth with ever greater depth and riches—with ever greater strictness of inevitable logic—had furrowed the brow, the cheeks, the mouth. When his mind was slumbering, the features appeared old and withered; when it awoke, they expressed all the earnestness and strength of a thought, which, through the persistent effort of years, had been developed to completeness. What dignity lay in the whole head, in the finely formed nose, the high but somewhat retreating brow, the peaceful chin! The nobleness of good faith and thorough rectitude in great and little, the clear consciousness of having sought satisfaction in truth alone, was, in the most individual way, imprinted on every feature. I had expected a testing and inspiring discourse about philosophy, and was mightily surprised to hear nothing of the kind.

Just returned from a tour in the Netherlands, Hegel would talk of nothing but the cleanliness of the cities, the charm and artificial fertility of the country, the green far-stretching meadows, the ponds, canals, tower-like mills, and well-made roads, the art treasures, and the formal but comfortable manner of living of the citizens; so that after half an hour I felt myself as much at home in Holland as with himself.

"When, after a few days, I saw him again in the professorial chair, I could not at first accommodate myself either to the manner of his outward address or the inward sequence of his thoughts. There he sat, with relaxed, half-sullen air, and, as he spoke, kept turning backwards and forwards the leaves of his long folio manuscript; a constant hacking and coughing disturbed the even flow of speech; every proposition stood isolated by itself, and seemed to force its way out all broken and twisted; every word, every syllable was, as it were, reluctantly let go, receiving from the metallic ring of the broad Swabian dialect a strange emphasis, as if *it* were the most important thing to be said. Yet the whole appearance compelled such deep respect, such a feeling of reverence, and attracted by such a *naïve* expression of overpowering earnestness, that, with all my discomfort, and though I may have understood little enough of what was said, I felt myself irresistibly bound to him. And no sooner, by zeal and patience, had I accustomed myself to these outward defects of his address, than they and its inward merits seemed to unite themselves into an organic whole, which claimed to be judged by itself alone.

"An easy-flowing eloquence presupposes that one has made up one's final accounts with the matter in hand, and therefore an ability of a merely formal kind is able to chatter away with cheap attractiveness, without rising above the region of commonplace. Hegel's work, on the other hand, was to call up the most powerful thoughts out of the deepest ground of things, and to bring them as living forces to bear upon his audience; and for this it was necessary that,—often as they had been meditated and recast through past years,— at every new expression they should be reproduced afresh in himself. A more vivid and plastic representation of this hard conflict and birth-labour of thought than Hegel's manner of address could not be conceived. As the oldest prophets, the more vehemently they struggle with language, utter with the more concentrated force that thought which they half conquer, and which half conquers them, so did he struggle and overcome by the unwieldy *verve* of his expression. Entirely lost in his subject, he seemed to develop it out of itself for its own sake, and scarcely at all for the sake of the hearer; and an almost paternal anxiety for clearness softened the rigid earnestness which otherwise might have repelled one from the reception of such hard-won thoughts. Stammering already at the beginning, he forced his way on, made a new beginning, again stopped short, spoke and meditated: the exact word seemed ever to be in request, and just then it came with infallible certainty. . . . Now one felt one had grasped a proposition, and expected a further advance to be made. In vain. The thought, instead of advancing, kept turning with similar words again and again round the same point. Yet if the wearied attention was allowed to stray for a moment, one found, on returning, that one had lost the thread of the discourse. For slowly and carefully, by apparently insignificant intermediate steps, a thought had been made to limit itself so as to show its one-sidedness, had been broken up into differences and entangled in contradictions, the solution of which suddenly brought what seemed most opposed to a higher reunion. And thus, ever carefully resuming again what had been gone over before, and deepening and transforming it by new divisions and richer reconciliations, the wonderful stream of thought flowed on, twisting and struggling with itself, now isolating and now uniting, now delaying and now springing forward with a leap, but always steadily moving to its goal. Even one who could follow with full insight and intelligence, without looking to the right or to the left, saw himself thrown into the most strange tension and agony of mind. To such depths was thought carried down, to such infinite oppositions was it torn asunder, that all that had been won seemed ever again to be lost, and after the highest effort the intelligence seemed to be forced to stand in silence at the bounds of its faculty. But it was just in these depths of the apparently undecipherable that that powerful spirit lived and moved with the greatest certainty and calm. Then first his voice rose, his eye glanced sharply over the audience, and lighted up with the calmly glowing flame of conviction, while in words that now flowed without hesitation, he measured the heights and depths of the soul. What he uttered in such moments was so clear and exhaustive, of such simple self-evidencing power, that every one who could grasp it felt as if he had found and thought it for himself; and so completely did all previous ways of thinking vanish, that scarce a remembrance remained of the days of dreaming, in which such thoughts had not yet been awakened.

". . . From his earliest youth Hegel had given himself with unwearied rectitude of purpose to every kind of scientific study; in later years he had lived for a time, like Schiller, estranged from the world, almost as in a cloister, while the impulse towards active life was fermenting within him. When he emerged from retirement, life subjected him to a hard school, outward embarrassments hemmed him in on all sides; and clearly as he saw the necessity of a complete remoulding of science, yet at that time he was far from feeling in himself the power to achieve such a reform by his own efforts. For he was one of those strong natures which only after a long process of growth, in the full maturity of manhood, reveal all their depth, but which then bring to the riper completion what has been so long developed in silence. When I first knew him his main works were published, his fame stood high, and also in all externals his position was fortunate. This comfort and peace lent to his whole bearing — except when his temper was fretted or blunted by bodily suffering — the most thorough kindliness. How gladly I met him on his daily walks; though he seemed to move forward with effort and without spring, he was really more robust and forcible than we younger men. He was ready for every pleasure-party,—nay, complete relaxation seemed, with advancing years, to have become more and more necessary to him. Who would then have recognised in him the deepest spirit of his time? Ever ready for talk, he rather sought to avoid, than to encourage, scientific subjects: the day's gossip, the *on dits* of the city, were welcome to him; political news, the art of the moment, came in for a share of his attention; and as his aim was amusement and recreation, he often approved at such moments what at other times he would have blamed, defended what he had before rejected, and found no end of chaffing me for my judicial strictness and straitness. What life there was in him at such times! Yet if one walked beside him, there was no getting on; for at every other moment he stood still, spoke, gesticulated, or sent forth a hearty ringing laugh; and whatever he might say, even when it was untenable and spoken to provoke contradiction, one was tempted to agree with him, so clearly and vigorously was it expressed. An equally agreeable companion he was at concerts and theatres—lively, inclined to applaud, ever ready for talk and jest, and content even, when it came to that, with the commonplaces of good society. Especially was he easy to please with his favourite singers, actresses, and poets. In business, on the other hand, his sharp understanding made him so painfully exact in weighing every *pro* and *con*, so scrupulous and obstinate, that men of quick decisive ways were often driven to despair by him; yet, if he had once resolved, his firmness was immovable. For in practical matters he had no want of insight; only the execution was difficult for him, and the smaller the matter the more helpless he was. Repellent personalities, who were opposed to the whole direction of his efforts, he could not abide, especially when their want of a fixed way of thinking had pained him in regard to that which he revered most: only in his most happy moods could one induce him to have any relations with such people. But when friends gathered round him, what an attractive loving *camaraderie* distinguished him from all others! The minute *nuance* of manners was not in his way; but a certain somewhat ceremonious *bourgeois* frankness united itself so happily, with jest where jest was in place, with earnest where the occasion required earnestness, and always with an equable good-humour, that all those surrounding him were instinctively drawn into the same tone. He was fond of the society of ladies; and where he knew them well, the fairest were always sure of a sportive devotion, which, in the pleasant security of approaching age, had maintained the freshness of youth. The greater the retirement in which his earlier laborious years had passed away, the greater was his pleasure in later days to live in society; and as if his own depth needed to find a compensation in the triviality or commonplace of others, at times he took pleasure in people of the commonest stamp, and even seemed to cherish for them a kind of good-humoured preference. With what natural dignity, on the other hand, and with what unaffected earnestness, did he appear when some public occasion made it necessary for him to come forward! And how many long hours of advice, of testing, of confirmation, was he ready to devote to those who sought his aid and guidance! If Plato celebrates how Socrates at the banquet preserved complete sobriety and measure even in the full tide of enjoyment, and when all the others were sleeping around, continued with Aristophanes and Agathon to drink and philosophise, till he left them overcome at cock-crow, and went out to the Lyceum to spend the day as usual, and only at the second evening cared to lay himself down to rest—I may surely say that Hegel alone, of all men whom I have seen, brought before my eyes this image of joyous, untiring energy, with a vivid force of realisation that can never be forgot."[1]

Hegel's life at Berlin was not very fertile in direct literary effort, though it was there for the most part that those lectures were produced and delivered which form the greater part of his published works. Besides the 'Philosophy of Right,' during this period two more

[1] Hotho, Vorstudien für Leben und Kunst, pp. 383-399.

editions of the 'Encyclopædia,' the last with considerable alterations, were given to the world, and the first volume of the 'Logic' was thoroughly revised. And in 1827, the Berlin Jahrbücher for Scientific Criticism, which were in the main, though not entirely, an organ of the Hegelian school, began to be issued; and to this Hegel during the following years contributed a number of important articles.

In 1830 he was chosen Rector of the University; and the festival of the third centenary of the Augsburg Confession gave him an opportunity again to declare his adherence to the "Standard of the Free Spirit," set up by Luther. The same year brought the July Revolution in Paris, and troubled him, as it troubled Niebuhr and many others, with the fear that France was again about to set the world on fire. This feeling shortly after found its expression in an article written on the English Reform Bill of 1831. In this article there are many severe criticisms on the English constitution, which had much justification then, and have not altogether ceased to be applicable now. But the main point lies in the distinction between "formal" and "real" freedom—in other words, between popular government and rational institutions, with which Hegel apparently seeks to console his countrymen for the slow development of the former in Prussia. The "ungodly jungle" of English law, the semi-feudal arrangements of landed inheritance, the power of the hereditary aristocracy, the abuses of the English Church, and in connection with this, the English tendency to treat public offices as private property, are compared with the more rational system introduced into these matters in Prussia by the Crown acting through enlightened ministers and civil servants; and Hegel is too near the French Revolution not to have many fears about a system like the English, in which the movement of reform cannot be initiated by the Crown, — which has lost all real power, — but must be won by the struggle of popular forces against a privileged aristocracy. Yet he sees the inevitableness of the change embodied in the Reform Bill, and points to the English experience of municipal self-government as a security against the dangers of revolutionary principles. The sagacity of many of Hegel's remarks has been proved by the subsequent history of the political movement in this country; what is defective in them is mainly due to the want of a living experience of the working of a free state, and perhaps also of a closer view of the English character. It is noticeable that even the moderate liberalism of this paper was too much for the growing fears of the Prussian Government, and a second part of it, which Hegel was preparing, was stopped by the censor.

This article was Hegel's last work, if we except a preface to the new edition of his 'Logic,' which ends somewhat sadly with an admission of the defects of his own development of the great principle of his philosophy, and an expression of his fear that the interval of political quiet, which had given such a favourable opportunity for philosophical culture, had come to an end. "One who has taken for his task to develop for the first time an independent structure of philosophical science in these latter days, must be reminded of the story that Plato wrote and rewrote his 'Republic' seven times over. This remembrance, and the comparison it suggests, might well awake a desire that, for a work which, as belonging to the modern world, has to deal with a harder subject, and to work upon a material of much greater compass, there might be given time to write and rewrite it even seventy times and seven. But while he thus thinks of the greatness of the task, the writer must content himself with what it has been allowed him to attain under the pressure of circumstances, under the unavoidable dissipation of energy caused by the greatness and many-sidedness of the interests of the times, and with haunting presence of a doubt whether, amid the loud noises of the day, and the deafening babble of vain opinion that cares for nothing but noise, there is left any room for sympathy with the passionless stillness of a science of pure thought."

Seven days after these words, weighty with the melancholy of genius, were written, Hegel was struck down by a sudden attack of cholera. This pestilence had been raging in Berlin during the summer, and had caused him to withdraw his family to a country house in the neighbourhood, and during the vacation almost to break off all connection with the city. But in the week previous to his death he had returned to his work, and had begun his lectures, on Thursday and Friday, the 10th and 11th of November, with a fire and energy of expression which surprised his hearers, and in which there was, perhaps, something of the false strength of disease. On Saturday he still did some university duties; but on Sunday he was suddenly seized by the cholera in its most virulent form, and the next day passed away in a quiet sleep, without having ever felt an apprehension of danger. He was buried in a spot which he himself had chosen, beside Solger, and Fichte, his great predecessor. "His death," wrote Varnhagen von Ense, "was as fortunate as death can ever be. With unweakened spirit, in vigorous activity, at the height of his fame and influence, surrounded by the proofs of his success, content with his position, taking a lively share in the social pleasures and showing a friendly sympathy in all the life of the capital,—he passed away from the midst of all these interests without regret or pain; for the nature and name of his illness remained unknown to him, and he might fall asleep with the dream of recovery. But for us, what an awful void! he was the corner-stone of our university."

Of Hegel's personal character and genius it is not necessary to add much to what has already been said. What strikes us most in his life, as in his philosophy, is the combination of a deeply idealistic, poetical, and religious view of the world, with that practical good sense and that critical keenness of understanding which are usually the possession of another order of minds. The inner life of pious feeling, the subtle suggestions of art, all the forms in which poetry, religion, and philosophy have expressed men's consciousness of the infinite, were open secrets to him, and it was in this element that he lived and moved with the utmost freedom. But though his greatest strength lay in his imaginative and speculative grasp of the things of the spirit, it was not as an idealistic, still less as a poetic genius that he impressed most of the immediate observers of his life. Until a comparatively late period, when growing clearness of self-consciousness had brought with it greater freedom of utterance, he was generally regarded rather as a man of strong understanding and definite practical aims, without superstitions or illusions of any sort. At college his most intimate friends evidently looked upon him as a good-humoured and reasonable companion, whose premature sobriety of judgment was inconsistent with any idea of genius. Even at a much later date the poet Hölderlin, who knew him as well as any one, calls him a "man of calm prosaic understanding" (*ruhiger Verstandesmensch*); and Schelling,—though this, it is true, was after his breach with Hegel—writes of him to the same effect. "Such a pure example of inward and outward prose must be held sacred in these our over-poetic days: for all of us have now and again a touch of sentimentality, and against this such a 'spirit that denies'[1] is an excellent corrective." In these words there is, indeed, a certain one-sidedness of judgment, which can only be explained as personal bitterness—for, after the 'Phænomenology,' it was absurd to speak of Hegel as essentially prosaic; yet there is probably also a recurrence to what was really the first impression produced by Hegel on one whose weakness was, that he never could understand the requirements of prose.

Now this view of Hegel's nature and tendencies was undoubtedly and entirely erroneous. The critical understanding—that sense of finite conditions which is the essence of prose, and which constitutes what is called a *positive* temper of mind in science or practical life—was powerfully developed in Hegel. But it was by no means

[1] An allusion to the description of Mephistopheles in 'Faust.'

the predominant characteristic of his genius, as we see it in his works. There are, however, reasons why it should have seemed to be so to those who looked at Hegel from the outside. One is that, though he was certainly not prosaic, he was almost entirely without an element which is most commonly mistaken for poetry, and which, in the passage just quoted, Schelling seems to confuse with it. To the impression of the beautiful and the ideal he was always open, and as we have seen, his whole thought was for a long period moulded by the influence of Greek art and literature. But he was not *sentimental*, and he even had a dislike of the "effusions of sensibility," which is rather uncommon in a German, and which must have been still more uncommon in the age of Werther. Hence he seems to have affected his countrymen somewhat in the same way that the manner of Englishmen usually affects them, as showing a lack in sympathy and spontaneity, and also—such is the natural judgment of less reserved natures—of poetic feeling. Yet the history of literature does not show that the native springs of imaginative feeling and expression are less genuine and copious in England than in Germany. And of few men could it be said with more certainty that he had "music in his soul," than of the author of the 'Phænomenology' and the 'Lectures on Æsthetic.'

Another characteristic of Hegel was closely connected with this want of what is technically called "sensibility." He never "made his studies in public," or in any way gave his thoughts to the world till they were ripe. Scarcely even did he communicate them to his most intimate friends. The important studies of his youth on the history and nature of religion, of which some account has been given in a previous chapter, were probably never heard of by any one till they were brought to light by his biographer: and it is most likely that, to his friends as to the public, his published writings were the first revelation of a speculative genius whose depth and riches they had scarcely even suspected. In society Hegel sought for relaxation, for extraneous interests which might break the tension of the inner life of thought; and except, perhaps, for a short time during his alliance with Schelling, he never really philosophised *with* any one—never developed his speculations by the living interchange of ideas, but always by solitary meditation. "In no pursuit," he says and repeats several times, "is one so solitary as in philosophy;" and this is specially true of his own philosophic life, which always went on below the surface as a hidden process of brooding thought, and seldom showed itself to others except in the completed result. Hence those who witnessed the outward life of the diligent tutor, or editor, or schoolmaster, or even those, in later days, who met Hegel at the whist-table or in the theatre, or listened, in general society, to his ready talk about art and politics, and indeed about everything except philosophy, might not suspect that they had seen almost nothing of the man. It was only in his direct work as a writer and teacher of philosophy that the inner life of thought—which with him was almost everything—freely revealed itself. And even in his professorial teaching it revealed itself so simply and directly,—working on the hearers entirely by its own power and not by any of the arts of the orator,—that the essential depth and earnestness of his character, as well as the poetic insight which was, so to speak, held in solution by the scientific strictness of his method, were apparent only to the few.

Hegel's style is, in many ways, a mirror of his mind. It may be described as a good style spoiled by the desire of scientific completeness and accuracy, and by the very weight of concentrated meaning which it is forced to convey. This, indeed, is no more than the fact; for his earlier writing—*e.g.*, in the unpublished treatise on the relations of positive and natural religion—has an ease and flow which is wanting to his later works. In the 'Phænomenology' there is already a good deal of that "repulsive terminology" which has often been complained of by those who will not recognise that it is almost as difficult to put metaphysical, as to put physical, science into the language of literature. Yet not only in that treatise, which is Hegel's literary masterpiece, but also in nearly all his works, when the subject allows of it, there are long passages which, for *verve* and beauty of expression, challenge comparison with the masters of style. Nor, even in his most abstruse works, can one read many pages without coming upon some of those powerful epigrammatic sayings, lighted up at once with dialectic and poetry, with which he loves to clench his argument. Generally, however, the stress of thought, and the effort to fix it in definite formulas, is too great to permit anything like pure literary form; and it is only on a second or third reading that we become aware of the living flowers of imagination which are scattered among the hard stones of the road over which we have been carried. The harshness and abstruseness of philosophical terminology, and the painfully subtle movement of an endless dialectic, are almost all that is at first seen by the student; and it is only when he learns how to break through this outward husk that he is able to reach the kernel of truth—truth poetical as well as philosophical—which it conceals.

CHAPTER VI.

THE PROBLEM OF PHILOSOPHY—STATEMENT OF IT BY KANT, FICHTE, SCHELLING, AND HEGEL.

It is the peculiar strength of the modern time that it has reached a clear perception of the finite world as finite; that in science it is positive—*i.e.*, that it takes particular facts for no more than they are; and that in practice it is unembarrassed by superstition—*i.e.*, by the tendency to treat particular things and persons as mysteriously sacred. The first immediate awe and reverence, which arose out of the confusion of the absolute and universal with the relative and particular, or, in simpler language, of the divine with the human, the ideal with the real, has passed away from the world. The artist and the poet, indeed, still keep up the confusion or identification; it is their work to give

> " To one brief moment caught from fleeting time
> The appropriate calm of blest eternity."

But we no longer take the artist or poet as a prophet; we cannot seriously and permanently worship the objects which he makes us admire. Whenever the evanescent light "that never was on sea or land" fades away from them, we are obliged to see that it never was there, and to treat the things and beings on which it fell as merely individual things and beings, like the things and beings around them. We are unable to believe in a God who is here and not there, in an ideal which is a happy exception. And the poet's vision, therefore, will necessarily become to us a dream, if it is not conceived as pointing to something more universal, of which he does not speak. The scientific sense, which has gradually communicated itself even to many of those who are not scientific, forces us to see in particular things not ideals, but merely examples of general classes, and to regard them all as connected to each other by laws of necessary relation, in such a way that they are *ipso facto* deprived of any exceptional or independent position. How can we treat anything as deserving of praise or worship for itself, if, to explain it, we have to look, not to itself, but to its conditions and causes? And when science bids us treat *everything* in this manner, how can there be anything left to reverence? "Zeus is dethroned, and Vortex reigns in his place."[1] Nor can we count it a more respectable worship when we are told to adore the unknown, which always lies at the end of every finite series of causes and effects, so long as no reason is given to suppose that what lies beyond our knowledge is other than a continuation of the chain that lies within it. The undeveloped terms of an infinite mathematical series have no preference over those that have been ascertained, and we cannot find any special reason for admiration in the fact that the series cannot be completed. An endless stream of finites is the negation of all worship, and it does not matter whether we regard its endlessness or

[1] Aristophanes, "Nubes," 381, 828.

the finitude of its parts. To find an object of reverence, we must be able in some way or other to rise to an original source of life, out of which this manifold existence flows, and which, in all this variety and change, never forgets or loses itself. A world of endless determination is a prosaic world, into which neither poetry nor religion can enter. To rise to either, we must find that which is self-determined,—we must have shown to us a fountain of fresh and original life. When we have found *that*, the multiplicity of forms, the endless series of appearances, will begin to take an ideal meaning, because we shall see in them the Protean masks of a Being which is never absolutely hidden, but in the perishing of one form and the coming of another is ever more fully revealing itself. It is by this suggestion of such a self-revealing unity that Goethe at a touch gives poetic life to the picture of change which modern science has set before us:—

> " In the floods of life, in the storm of deeds,
>   Up and down I fly,
>   Hither, thither weave,
>   From birth to grave,
>   An endless weft,
>   A changing sea
>   Of glowing life.
>   Thus in the whistling loom of Time I ply,
>   Weaving the living robe of Deity."

The great question of philosophy is whether such a unity in totality, such a self-determined principle of infinite change, can in any sense be verified, or made an object of knowledge. And this for us is so difficult a question, just because the modern consciousness of the natural world, as an interconnection of phenomenal causes, is so clear and precise. No longer is it possible, as it once was, to intercalate the ideal, the divine, as it were surreptitiously, as one existence in a world otherwise secular and natural. Under the acknowledged reign of law, the world is a connected drama in which there is no place for episodes. Hence we can find the ideal anywhere, only by finding it everywhere; we can see anything higher in the world than contingent and finite existences, only by recasting our view of it as a whole; we can get beyond the scientific conception of phenomena in their connection as causes and effects, only by transforming that conception itself, by awakening science to a new consciousness of its presuppositions, and by leading it through this consciousness to a reinterpretation of its results. It no longer avails to assail finite science from the outside, in the way of finding exceptions to its laws, or phenomena which it cannot explain. A long discipline has taught it to regard such exceptional or residual phenomena simply as the means of correcting and widening its ideas of law. If it is assailable at all, it is from the inside, in its fundamental conception of law itself,—in its idea of that universal necessity under which it reduces all things.

Now the great idealistic movement of Germany was, in its essence, an attempt to find a basis of this kind. Kant, its first representative, asked where a place can be found for "God, freedom, immortality," consistently with the universal reign of law in the natural world— in other words, consistently with the necessary connection of all objects of experience in space and time. Nor did he seek to find such a place by questioning the universality of this necessary interdependence of all things and events; rather he reasserted it, and finally confirmed it, by the proof that such universality is the precondition of all intelligible experience. Objects, things, and events—a world of experience—exist for us, and can exist for us, only in so far as our sensitive impressions are determined and related to each other according to universal principles. Objectivity and universality are equivalents of each other, and to say that an object might exist which was not definitely determined as to its quality and quantity, or definitely related to all other objects in space and time both in its persistence and in its changes, is to use words without meaning. If we could imagine such an object — or, what is the same thing, if we could imagine a series of impressions or perceptions which yet it was impossible to bring under the general laws of the connection of experience—we should be conceiving of something inconsistent with the very existence of experience. If there were such objects, they could not be objects *for us*.

While, however, the reign of law is thus determined to be absolute for all objects of experience, and while the principle of rational empiricism, that there exists a universal and unchangeable order of things, is thus raised from a presumption to a certitude, it is just here, at the point where the last possibility of escape from the necessity of nature seems to be closed up, that Kant finds the means of deliverance. This order of nature, which seems to shut us in, is no foreign necessity to which we are subjected. It is we who forge our own chains. It is our own understanding that prescribes the law of necessary connection for its objects, as it is our own sensibility

Nature and Freedom. 117

that supplies the forms of time and space under which they appear to us. In so far, therefore, as the general framework or systematic form of the whole goes, it is we who make the nature by which we fear to have our freedom, our spiritual life, or independent self-determining energy, extinguished. And as it is just this general systematic form in which lies the necessity from which we are shrinking, it may be said in strict truth that we are afraid of our own shadow,—of that which the unconscious working of our own minds has created. What we took for "things in themselves," independent forces by which we were controlled, are really *phenomena*—things which exist only for us, and which exist, even for us, only by the activity of our own thought. It is true, indeed, that we too form, in one point of view, a part of this phenomenal world; we are present to ourselves as objects existing, like other objects, in space and time, and going through changes which are determined according to necessary laws. But this phenomenal presence to ourselves is not our whole being. I am not merely one object among many other objects in the world of which I am conscious; I am the conscious self without which there would be no world of objects at all. A conscious being, as such, cannot simply reckon itself among the things it knows, for while they exist only for it, it also exists for itself. It not only has a place among objects, but it is the subject for which they exist. As such it is not one of the conditioned substances in time and space, whose changes are to be explained by the things that condition it; it is the principle in relation to which such conditioned things exist, the cause of the necessity to which they are subjected.

It is not in time and space at all, for these are but the forms of its perceptions—forms which cling to its objects *as* objects, but cannot be applied to it, the subject for which these objects exist. The source of the categories —the principles of necessary connection in experience— cannot be brought under the categories. The thinking self cannot be subjected to the forms of sense under which the phenomenal world is presented to it. Even if we could say nothing else about it, we could at least deny of it all the predicates which are by their very nature determinations not of a subject, but of an object.

But can we say nothing else? Is the subject a mere unity to which knowledge is referred, and which, therefore, is not only exempted from all the determinations of objects, but is void of all determination of its own? Can we say only that it is free in the *negative* sense, that that necessity of relation which belongs to phenomena, as such, cannot be predicated of it, seeing it determines other things, but not itself? Or can we go on to show that it is free in the *positive* sense, that it determines itself, and can we follow it in this self-determination, and trace out the forms in which it manifests its freedom? The answer, Kant holds, is given by the moral consciousness, which is a consciousness of ourselves as universal subjects, and not as particular objects. This is shown by the fact that conscience ignores all external determination. It is the consciousness of a law which takes no account of the circumstances of the phenomenal self, or of the necessary conditions under which its changes take place. In thinking of ourselves as under this law, we necessarily regard ourselves as free—as the authors, and the sole authors, of our actions; we abstract from all the limits of nature and necessity—from all the impulse of desires within, and all the pressure of circumstances without us. For this law is a "categorical imperative" that listens to no excuses, but with its "Thou oughtst, therefore thou canst," absolutely throws upon ourselves the responsibility for our own deeds. Such a law we might be disposed to treat as an illusion, because of its direct contradiction to our empirical consciousness of ourselves, if we had no other consciousness of ourselves; but our previous examination of the empirical consciousness has already obliged us to refuse to apply to the *subject* the knowledge which we have of ourselves as *objects* of experience. The necessity of nature is thus taken out of the way by the proof that the knowing self is not a natural phenomenon, and the moral consciousness finds nothing to resist its absolute claim to belief and obedience. The "primacy of practical reason" is thus established, and a place is found for the freedom of spirit, without any doubt being cast upon the necessity of nature.

And with this freedom come, according to Kant, the other elements of our higher consciousness—immortality and God. For the primacy of the practical reason involves that the necessity of nature is somehow harmonised with the law of freedom, however little it may be possible for us to comprehend this harmony. Hence the phenomenal self—the subject of feeling and desire —must conform itself to the real or noumenal self; and the pure *self*-determination of the latter must determine also the whole nature of the former. But we are not able to represent this to ourselves except as a gradual process of transformation of our sensuous nature by our freedom,—a process of transformation which, because of the essential difference of the two, can never be completed; and thus the moral law postulates the immortality of man as a subject, who is at once natural and moral. In like manner we are compelled, in accordance with the primacy of practical reason, to suppose that the whole system of phenomena which we call nature is in harmony with the purely self-determined life of spirit; in other words, we are obliged to assume a correspondence of happiness, or our state as natural beings determined from without, with goodness, or our state as moral beings, who are determined only by themselves from within; and this, again, leads us back to God as the absolute Being, in whom, and by whom, the two opposite worlds are brought to a unity. Thus, then, Kant finds a way of reconstructing the spiritual, without prejudice to the natural, world. For if, on the one hand, the world of nature is treated as phenomenal, while the world of spirit is regarded as the real, and the only real, world; yet, on the other hand, the phenomenal world is recognised as the only world of knowledge, while the real world is said to be present to us merely in faith. Now faith is essentially a *subjective* consciousness, which cannot be made objective; for to make anything objective is to conceive it as a one thing among others in space and time, and determined in relation to the others by the law of necessity. So much is this the case, that we are not able to represent to ourselves the law of freedom except by thinking of it as if it were a law of nature. For what is the law of freedom? It is that we should be determined only by the self; but the self is nothing in particular; it is the unity to which all knowledge is referred; its only essential character is its universality. Hence, to be determined by the self is to be determined by the idea of universality. To find out what is morally right, we have only to ask what actions may be universalised, and the moral law may be expressed in the formula: "Act as if by your action the maxim or rule which it involves were about to be turned into a universal law of nature."

Without following Kant any further, it is possible now to point out what are the merits and what are the defects of his philosophy, viewed as a reconciliation of nature and spirit, or of experience and that higher rational consciousness which is expressed in religion and philosophy. Its main merit is, that it shows that experience rests on something which, in the ordinary sense, is beyond experience; or, what is the same thing in another point of view, that it brings out the relativity of being to thought,—of objective reality to the conscious self for which it is. In this point of view—in so far as it shows that reality as known is phenomenal, or essentially related to consciousness, the Kantian argument is irresistible. Its weakness lies in this, that it does not carry the demonstration to its legitimate result; it still retains the idea of a "thing in itself," out of relation to thought, even where it regards such a thing as problematical; and it admits the idea of a subjective affection, in relation to which the thinking self is passive, though it confesses that it is only by the reaction of the thinking self that such an affection can be turned into an object of knowledge. Through the rift of this πρῶτον ψεῦδος there creeps into the system an absolutely irreconcilable dualism, which yet Kant is continually attempting to heal. Sense and understanding, necessity and freedom, the phenomenal and the real self, nature and spirit, knowledge and faith, are pairs of opposites which he can never either separate or reconcile. He cannot separate them, for his whole philosophy starts from the proof that nature is phenomenal, and must be referred to that which is not itself natural; and, on the other hand, he necessarily conceives the noumenal—that which is set up against the phenomenal—as the absolutely real, and as determining, and in a sense including in itself, the phenomenal. Yet he cannot reconcile them; for he has assumed, to begin with, that there is in the object as opposed to the subject, in sense as opposed to spirit, a foreign element which can never be exorcised or completely assimilated, although both in knowledge and in action it may be partially subdued and subordinated. The antithesis has thus no higher unity beyond it, which can bring its antagonistic members to a final reconciliation; and that reunion of these members, therefore, which is, after all, necessary to the system, must remain a postulate or requirement, which cannot be realised—which can even be seen to be incapable of realisation. The result of Kant, therefore, seems to be to put the very problem to be solved for the solution,—to show the equal necessity of two elements, which are each of them proved to have no meaning except in relation to the other, while yet this relation is conceived as *purely negative*, and therefore—since a purely negative relation is no relation at all—as absolutely impossible.

It was perhaps just because a consciousness of this truth—that a relation, even if negative, always implies a unity beyond it—was wanting to Kant, that he could admit the necessary relation of physical and metaphysical reality to each other, while yet denying the possibility of reaching more than an external harmony between them. Yet it is clear, to consider only Kant's first principle, that to say that existence means *existence for consciousness*, implies not merely that there is a relation between consciousness on the one side and existence on the other (in which case the relation would exist, not for the conscious being himself, but for some one else), but it implies also that consciousness transcends the dualism between itself and its object. It means, in short, that though, within certain limits, we oppose the subject to the object, the consciousness to that of which it is conscious, yet that from a higher point of view this antagonism is *within* consciousness; or, to put it from the other side, that consciousness, as such, overreaches the division between itself and its object. And the same reasoning must be applied to all the other contrasts which in the system of Kant spring out of this fundamental opposition—the contrasts of necessity and freedom, of nature and spirit, of phenomenal and noumenal. A philosophy that would work out the true lesson of the Kantian idealism must not weaken or slur over any of these oppositions; but as little can it deal with them as absolute oppositions, or, what is the same thing, treat the two terms as both standing on the same level, as if the one were as comprehensive as the other. For if it does so, it must necessarily end by contradicting the premises from which it starts, by refusing to admit any relation between terms, whose relation was the very starting-point of the whole reasoning. One who, like Kant, refers nature to spirit, necessity to freedom, the phenomenon to the noumenon, must be prepared to explain the former out of the latter; in the language of Hegel, to show that spirit is the *truth* of nature, that freedom is the *truth* of necessity, that the noumenon is the *truth* of the phenomenon —*i.e.*, that in spite of their relative opposition, there is a point of view from which the former term in each case includes the latter, as the whole includes the parts. Or, to take the example already given, he must show that consciousness, though it may be primarily regarded as the subject of knowledge, is not simply opposed to the object, but necessarily includes it in itself.

To gather to a point what has just been said, Kant proves that the system of nature and necessity is not independent of intelligence, but exists only for it. But the intelligence is not only consciousness, but self-consciousness—not only theoretical, but practical. It not only *is* determined, and so apprehends itself as belonging to the world of nature, but it determines itself, and so is conscious of itself as belonging to a world of its own—a world of freedom. And this world of freedom it is obliged to conceive as the reality, of which the other is merely the phenomenon. What Kant, however, does not perceive, is that, on his own showing, these two worlds are essentially relative to each other, so that either, taken apart from the other, becomes an empty abstraction. He has, indeed, proved that existence unrelated to a conscious self is such an abstraction. But it is clear that the pure self, in its universality—as opposed to all the matter of the desires—is equally abstract. To will the self, and only the self, is to will nothing at all. Self-consciousness always implies consciousness of something else than self, and could not exist without it. Self-determination, therefore, though it may be relatively opposed to determination by the not-self, cannot be absolutely opposed to it, for with the not-self the self also would disappear. But if this be true, the world of intelligence and freedom cannot be different from the world of nature and necessity; it can only be the same world, seen in a new light, or subjected to a further interpretation. And this new interpretation must show that the necessity of nature is itself explicable as a necessary element or factor in the manifestation of the principle of the free life of intelligence. Not, indeed, that the point of view of Kant, from which the two kingdoms of necessity and freedom seem to be in extreme opposition to each other, is to be entirely rejected. On the contrary, that opposition forms a necessary stage in thought and reality. The drama of human life is the struggle of freedom with necessity, of spirit with nature, which in all its forms, within and without us, seems to the purely moral consciousness to wear the guise of an enemy. But the possibility of the struggle itself, and of a final victory in it, lies in this, that the enemy exists in order to be conquered; or rather, that the opposition is, in its ultimate interpretation, an opposition of spirit to itself, and the struggle but the pains that accompany its process of development.

There are two bypaths in following which it is possible to lose the full meaning of the thought just expressed. On the one hand, it is possible to dwell on the higher reality of spirit in such a sense as not to leave due place for the lower reality of nature: it is possible to emphasise Kant's demonstration of the phenomenal character of the world of experience, till that world is reduced to a mere semblance or appearance, and to exaggerate his assertion of the noumenal character of the world of intelligence, till the pure abstract consciousness of self is identified with the absolute. On the other hand, it is possible to insist on the unity which is presupposed in all the opposition and antagonism of the nature and the spirit, till the opposition and antagonism itself is reduced to an illusion; it is possible, in other words, to treat all differences as mainly accidental shiftings of the external mask under which the absolute identity is hidden, and to regard all conflict and antagonism as but the play of shadows,—"such stuff as dreams are made of,"—while the one reality is the external repose of the infinite substance in itself. These two byways of interpretation — which are the natural results of a partial apprehension of the full problem stated by Kant—were followed by Fichte and Schelling respectively. Fichte, following the way of a one-sided idealism, reduces nature to a mere negative condition, which spirit—by some incomprehensible act — lays down for itself. To attain consciousness of itself, the absolute *ego* must limit itself, and by this self-limitation it gives rise to a *non-ego*, which, however, is quite as much a part of itself as the limited *ego*, with which alone it is consciously identified. The infinity of the *ego*, however, reappears as an impulse to strive against this self-made limit, and by continual removal of it to a greater and greater distance, to approximate to that pure consciousness of itself which it can never attain, because in doing so it would at once cease to be conscious at all, and so cease to be. This is the strange enchanted round, within which the speculation of Fichte circles, seeking an outlet in vain. In the attempt to reduce nature to a nonentity—a self-created object of thought—and to make spirit all in all, he turned the life of spirit itself into something shadowy and spectral,—a conflict with a ghost that could not be laid. To the strong, almost ascetic spirit of a Fichte, rejoicing in stern self-command to put nature beneath his feet, and regarding the world but as an arena for the moral athlete to win his victories over himself, such a theory might commend itself by its apparent exaltation of the *ego* at the expense of the *non-ego*. But we need not wonder that the sympathetic imaginative genius of Schelling soon broke away from it, to assert that the intelligence could find itself in nature as well as in itself: or that he sought to substitute for Fichte's principle that "Ich ist Alles," the wider principle that "Alles ist Ich"—*i.e.*, that it is one ideal principle which manifests itself in the natural and the spiritual world alike. Unfortunately, in correcting Fichte's over-statement of one of the two sides of the Kantian philosophy, Schelling fell into an equal over-statement on the other side. In opposing a subjective idealism which found reality only in the self, he was led, by gradual but necessary steps, to reject idealism altogether, and to seek the real in a coequal unity of nature and spirit, which gave no preference to the one above the other as a manifestation of the absolute. But to say that the absolute equally manifests itself in nature and spirit, is almost equivalent to saying that it does not manifest itself at all; for if the distinguishing characters of mind and matter are treated as unimportant, and their identity alone is insisted on, what distinctions *can* be of importance? The absolute unity becomes necessarily a pure "indifference," as Schelling called it, an absolute which rests in itself and withdraws itself from all contact with the intelligence, and which can be apprehended, if at all, only in a Neoplatonic ecstasy of immediate intuition. In this way Schelling, though content for a time, with Hegel, to speak of the absolute as spirit or reason, gradually withdrew from these words all their fulness of meaning, until it became necessary and just for Hegel to reassert against him the primitive lesson of Kantian philosophy, that "the absolute is not substance but subject"—*i.e.*, that the unity, to which all things are to be referred and in which they must find their ultimate explanation, is the unity of self-consciousness.

When, however, Hegel thus rejected both these partial solutions of the Kantian problem,—solutions which really involve the omission of one or other of its elements,—and when he again restated the problem itself in all its fulness, he could no longer, like Kant, escape from its difficulties by an alternation between intelligible and phenomenal reality, or between the spheres of reason and faith. For him it was necessary to show that the kingdoms of nature and spirit are one, in spite of all their antagonisms; nay, it was necessary for him to show that this antagonism itself is the manifestation of their unity. The freedom that belongs to man as a rational and moral being could no longer be saved by lifting it, as it were, into another world, a τόπος νοητός, out of the reach of physical necessity; it must be shown to realise itself in and through that necessity itself. "Out of the eater must come forth meat; out of the strong, sweetness." What had been regarded as absolute opposites or contradictories, mind and matter, spirit and nature, self-determination and determination by the not-self, must be united and reconciled, and that not by an external harmony, but by bringing out into distinct consciousness the unity that lies beyond their difference, and gives it its meaning. To do this, indeed, was to break with all the ideas of logical method that had hitherto ruled the schools; it was to treat as ultimately pliant and evanescent the most fixed distinctions of the old metaphysics. Yet it was not to be done, as it had often been done by mystics like Böhme and intuitionists like Jacobi, by simply rejecting the claims of the logical understanding to lay down any law for the higher matters of the spirit. Such a resource was not permitted to one who, like Hegel, declared that self-consciousness itself was the ideal unity, by which, or in reference to which, the world must be explained. In a philosophy that acknowledged such a principle, the movement of thought, by which the most fixed distinctions of the understanding were dissolved and its most absolute oppositions transcended, must be a logical movement, and it must be conscious of its own logic. Its "reason," to use a common distinction, must not be set against its "understanding," but must include and satisfy it. If its higher philosophical or religious truth was not brought down into the region of common-sense, at least it must gain a clear conscience toward common-sense by fulfilling all its reasonable demands, and leaving it no excuse to deny the rationality of that which transcended it. Especially must such a philosophy be ready to meet on its own ground that higher kind of common-sense called science; it must be scientific, even if it was necessary for it to be something more. It is this that makes Hegel so vehement in his opposition to all those who, like Schelling, lay claim to a special immediate vision or intellectual intuition of truth from which the mass of men are excluded. To those who quote the Scripture that "God giveth" truth "to his beloved in sleep,"[1] he is ready to assume the sceptical attitude of rationalism, and to point out that "what is given to men in sleep is for the most part dreams." Yet it is not in the interest of rationalism that Hegel speaks, but in the interest of that ideal truth which rationalism denies. But it is his inmost conviction that there are not two truths, but one, and that *that* is no secure path to a higher kind of knowledge, which begins by a quarrel with the facts of life and the ordinary consciousness of these facts. As the late Professor Green has said, that "there is no other genuine enthusiasm of humanity than one which has travelled the common highway of reason —the life of the good neighbour and honest citizen—and can never forget that it is only on a further stage of the same journey;" so, in Hegel's view, philosophy can permanently vindicate that highest synthesis which lifts thought from the finite to the infinite, only when it has fully recognised and done justice to the finite consciousness with which it starts. The claim of special inspira-

[1] Psalm cxxvii. 2—see German translation.

Idealism and Dualism. 131

tion is an anachronism for the modern spirit which demands that the saint should also be a man of the world, and that the prophet should show the logical necessity of his vision. For "a man's a man for a' that," and, however sensuous and rude his consciousness of himself and of the world may be, it is, after all, a rational consciousness, and it claims the royal right of reason to have its errors disproved out of itself. And a philosophy which does not find sufficient premises to prove itself in the intelligence of every one, and which is forced to have recourse to mere *ex cathedra* assertion, is confessing its impotence.

But this resolve to bring together poetry with prose, religion with experience, philosophy with the science of the finite, the "vision and the faculty divine" with common-sense and the natural understanding, obviously entails upon speculation a harder task than it has ever before encountered. Dualism in some form or other has for centuries lightened the task of philosophy by a sort of double book-keeping or division of labour, by which the hardest contrasts and antagonisms of life were evaded. Even for Kant, who brings the two worlds face to face, there is still a "great gulf fixed" between them, and moral freedom moves safely in a vacant "kingdom of ends," where it never comes in contact with any necessity of nature. But for Hegel, all such devices to keep the peace, so to speak, between heaven and earth—to put some interval of separation "between the pass and fell incensed points of mighty opposites"—are vain and fruitless. If the Kantian principle, that self-consciousness or self-determining spirit is the ultimate reality of things, is to be maintained, it must be shown to be a principle capable of explaining the phenomenal world. That very necessity of nature, from which Kant sought to find an escape for man's higher life, must be shown to be the means of realising it. How this is possible we shall consider afterwards; for the present it need only be remarked, that it is just Hegel's determination to avoid all shifts and subterfuges, — to encounter fairly all the difficulties of the spiritual or ideal interpretation of life, and to work out that interpretation faithfully even in those spheres which an ideal philosophy has not usually ventured to touch,—that forces him to deal with the problem of the reconciliation of opposites. It is no freak of an oversubtle logic, "trying for once in a way to stand on its head," that leads him to ask whether, beneath all the antagonisms of thought and reality, even those that have been hitherto conceived to be absolute contradictions, there is not a principle of unity, which in its development at once explains the opposition, shows its relative character and its limits, and finally dissolves it. This question was, in fact, forced on him by the gradual transformation of the Kantian philosophy in Fichte and Schelling. Their speculations made it manifest that the idealism of Kant could be maintained, only if self-consciousness were found to be a principle adequate to the explanation of that which is the very opposite of self-consciousness—*i.e.*, only if spirit could be shown to be the *reason* of nature, and mind to be the key to matter. And the apparent breach with common-sense which is involved in Hegel's denial of the law of contradiction as ordinarily understood, was the direct result of the very strength of common-sense in Hegel himself, which would not let him be content without bringing his highest spiritual consciousness into relation with the teachings of the ordinary understanding, and demanding that in one way or another the difference between the two should be brought to a definite issue.

CHAPTER VII.

THE PRINCIPLE OF CONTRADICTION AND THE IDEA OF SPIRIT.

WHEN Aristotle laid down the *Law of Contradiction* as the highest law of thought, and opposed it to the Heraclitean principle of universal flux, he argued that, unless distinction is maintained,—unless things are definitely what they are, and are kept to their definition,—knowledge and thought become impossible. If A and not-A are the same, it is no longer possible to find any meaning in the simplest statements. Even the doctrine of flux itself must mean something, and that obviously implies that it does not mean anything else; even the sceptic, therefore, when he assails the law of contradiction, tacitly gives in his adhesion to the truth he assails. To this argument no objection can be taken, if it be regarded as vindicating one necessary aspect or element of thought, and not as expressing its whole nature. Thought *is* always distinction, determination, the marking off of one thing from another; and it is characteristic of Aristotle—the great definer—that he should single out this aspect of it. But thought is *not only* distinction, it is at the same time *relation*. If it marks off one thing from another, it, at the same time, connects one thing with another. Nor can either of these functions of thought be separated from the other: as Aristotle himself said, the knowledge of opposites is one. A thing which has nothing to distinguish it is unthinkable, but equally unthinkable is a thing which is so separated from all other things as to have no community with them. If, therefore, the law of contradiction be taken as asserting the self-identity of things or thoughts in a sense that excludes their community—in other words, if it be *not* taken as limited by another law which asserts the relativity of the things or thoughts distinguished—it involves a false abstraction. A half-truth is necessarily distorted into a falsehood when taken as the whole truth. An *absolute* distinction by its very nature would be self-contradictory, for it would cut off all connection between the things it distinguished. It would annihilate the relation implied in the distinction, and so it would annihilate the distinction itself. If, therefore, we say that everything—every intelligible object or thought as such—must be differentiated from all others, yet we must equally say that no object or thought can be absolutely differentiated; in other words, differentiated so as to exclude any identity or unity which transcends the difference. An absolute difference is something which cannot exist within the intelligible world, and the thought which attempts to fix such a difference is unconscious of its own meaning. If it could succeed, it would, *ipso facto*, commit suicide. We can stretch the bow to the utmost point consistent with its not breaking, but if we go an inch further, it ceases to be stretched at all. We can embrace in one thought the widest antagonism consistent with the unity of thought itself, but an antagonism inconsistent with that unity is unthinkable, for the simple reason that, when the unity disappears, the antagonism also disappears with it.

If then the world, as an intelligible world, is a world of distinction, differentiation, individuality, it is equally true that in it, as an intelligible world, there are no absolute separations or oppositions, no antagonisms which cannot be reconciled. All difference presupposes a unity, and is itself, indeed, an expression of that unity; and if we let it expand and develop itself to the utmost, yet ultimately it must exhaust itself, and return into the unity. This is all that Hegel means when he, as is often asserted, "denies the validity of the laws of identity and contradiction." All he denies, in fact, is their *absolute* validity. "Every finite thing is itself, and no other." True, Hegel would answer, but with a *caveat*. Every finite thing, by the fact that it is finite, has an essential relation to that which limits it, and thus it contains the principle of its destruction in itself. It is therefore, in this sense, a self-contradictory existence, which at once is itself and its other, itself and not itself. It is at war with itself, and its very life-process is the process of its dissolution. In an absolute sense, it cannot be said *to be*, any more than *not to be*. "Every definite thought, by the fact that it is definite, excludes other thoughts, and especially the opposite thought." True, Hegel would answer, but with a *caveat*. Every definite thought, by the fact that it is definite, has a necessary relation to its negative, and cannot be separated from it without losing its own meaning. In the very definiteness with which it affirms itself, therefore, is contained the proof that its affirmation is not absolute. If we fix our attention upon it, to the exclusion of its negative, if we try to hold it to itself alone, it disappears. To maintain it and do it full justice is already to go beyond it. Hence we are obliged to modify the assertion, that every definite thought absolutely excludes its negative, and to admit that, in this point of view, it also includes or involves it. It is, and it is not, itself, for it contains in itself its own negation. If we are to reassert it again, it can only be so far as we combine it with its negative in a higher thought, in which, therefore, it is partly denied and partly affirmed.

Thus neither things nor thoughts can be treated as simply self-identical—as independent or atomic existences, which are related only to themselves. They are essentially parts of a whole, or stages in a process, and as such they carry us beyond themselves, the moment we clearly understand them. Nor can we escape from this conclusion by saying that it is merely a subjective illusion, and that the objects really remain, though our mind passes from the one to the other. In regard to thoughts, this is obviously a subterfuge; for the thought is not something different from the process which our minds go through in apprehending it—it *is* that process. And in regard to "things," the distinction is equally inapplicable; for what we are considering is the conditions essential to the intelligible, as such, and the " things " of which we speak must be at least intelligible, since they exist for our intelligence. The truth therefore is, that definiteness, finitude, or determination, as such, though they have an affirmative or positive meaning, also contain or involve in themselves their own negation. There is a community or unity between them and their opposites, which overreaches their difference or opposition, though it does not by any means exclude that difference or opposition *in its proper place, and within its proper limits.* Of any definite existence or thought, therefore, it may be said with quite as much truth that it *is not*, as that it *is*, its own bare self. This appears paradoxical, only because we are accustomed to think that the whole truth about a thing can be expressed once for all in a proposition; and here we find that two opposite propositions can be asserted with equal truth. The key, however, to the difficulty is, that neither the assertion nor the denial, nor even both together, exhaust all that is to be said. To know an object, we must follow the process of its existence, in which it manifests all that is in it, and so by that very manifestation exhausts itself, and is taken up as an element into a higher existence.

The thought that there is a unity which lies beneath all opposition, and that, therefore, all opposition is capable of reconciliation, is unfamiliar to our ordinary consciousness for reasons that may easily be explained. That unity is not usually an object of consciousness, just because it is the presupposition of all consciousness. It escapes notice, because it is the ground on which we stand, or the atmosphere in which we breathe; because it is not one thing or thought rather than another, but that through which all things are, and are known. Hence we can scarcely become conscious of its existence until something leads us to question its truth. Our life is an antagonism and a struggle, which rests upon a basis of unity, and would not be possible without it. But

Absolute Contradiction impossible. 139

immersed in the conflict, and occupied with our adversary, we cannot at the same moment rise to the consciousness of that power which is working in him and in us alike. Rather are we disposed to exaggerate the breadth of the gulf that separates us, and the intensity of the repulsion that sets us at war with each other. We disown the community that binds opposite ideas together, because we think that in no other way can we emphasise sufficiently our own watchword. We lose sight of truth itself, that we may assert *our* truth. Of this we may find examples in every sphere of life. Thus we find the scientific man exaggerating the contrasts of subjective and objective, thought and fact, to a point which would make all science unmeaning. The demand so often made, "Give us facts, and not hypotheses or ideas," does not mean what it says; for enough of facts may be collected—say, about the articles in a room, or the history of an hour's life in it—to break down the strongest memory. What it does mean is, "Give us facts that will answer the questions of our intelligence"—*i.e.*, facts that are ideas. But the scientific man feels so strongly the necessity of struggling against subjective opinions and "anticipations of nature" in his own mind and the minds of others in order that he may reach the objective truth, the ideas which are facts, that thought itself seems to be his enemy. In his struggle against "mere ideas," he loses sight of that ultimate unity of thought and things which is the presupposition of all his endeavours, and indeed the very principle which he is seeking to develop and to verify. It is, however, the moral and religious consciousness, which, just because its conflicts are those that most deeply divide us against ourselves and against each other, is most obstinate and stiff-necked in insisting on the absoluteness of its divisions and oppositions. Thus pious feeling is prone to exaggerate the division between divine and human, and even fears to admit the possibility of the intelligence of man apprehending in any sense the nature of God. "Our fittest eloquence is our silence when we confess without confession that Thy glory is inexplicable and beyond our reach." Such words may have a certain relative truth; but if we took them in their literal meaning,—that divine and human reason are different in kind, and that God cannot be known,—religion would be an impossibility. In like manner, the moral sense is jealous of the admission that good overreaches the antagonism between itself and evil, or in any sense comprehends, even if it be at the same time declared that it transcends, that antagonism: such an idea seems to it "a confusion of right and wrong." Yet the great moral teacher of our time, who above all has insisted that there is a hell as well as a heaven, is driven to meet what he thinks a superficial benevolence towards "scoundrels" with the cry, "Yes, they *are* my brethren, *hence this rage and sorrow!*" In other words, "Admit the antagonism which I assert in all its real depth and intensity, and I will admit that there is a unity beyond it." It is the unity itself which gives its bitter meaning to the difference, while at the same time it contains the pledge that the difference can and even must be reconciled.

"The intelligible world is relative to the intelligence." This principle, which was expressed by Kant, but of which Kant, by his distinctions of phenomenon and noumenon, reason and faith, evaded the full meaning, is taken in earnest by Hegel. He is therefore forced to deny the absoluteness even of those antagonisms which have been conceived to be altogether insoluble: for any absolute antagonism would ultimately imply an irreconcilable opposition between the intelligence and its object. In other words, it would imply that the intelligence is *not* the unity which is presupposed in all the differences of things, and which, therefore, through all these differences, returns to itself. The essential unity of all things with each other and with the mind that knows them, is the adamantine circle within which the strife of opposites is waged, and which their utmost violence of conflict cannot break. No fact, which is in its nature incapable of being explained or reduced to law,—no law, which it is impossible ever to recognise as essentially related to the intelligence that apprehends it,—can be admitted to exist in the intelligible universe. No absolute defeat of the spirit,—no defeat that does not contain the elements of a greater triumph,—can possibly take place in a world which is itself nothing but the realisation of spirit.

In a sense, this principle may be said to be incapable of proof, since a proof of it would already presuppose it. But a disproof of it would do so equally. And scepticism, when it brings this very result to light—in other words, when in its own necessary development it destroys itself—gives all the proof of it that is necessary. The self-contradiction of absolute scepticism makes us conscious of the unity of thought and things, of being and knowing, as an ultimate truth, which yet is not an assumption, because all belief and unbelief, all assertion and denial, alike presuppose it. The Kantian "transcendental deduction" was only a further, though still a partial, development of this idea; for it was an attempt to show what are the primary elements of thought involved in the determination of objects, as such; in other words, to show in detail what is meant by that identity or unity of the intelligence and its object, which is implied by all knowledge. As scepticism proved that to doubt the intelligence in *general* was suicidal, because with the intelligence disappears also the intelligible; so Kant's deduction proved that to take away any *special* part or form of the intelligence, any category of the understanding or form of sensibility, was to make knowledge impossible. Unfortunately, for reasons already indicated, Kant treats this unity as existing only in the phenomenal world of experience; and while he gives us a catalogue of the different elements out of which it is made up, he does not show how, in such diversity of operation, the intelligence can still be one, and conscious of itself as one. Kant, in other words, deals with the intelligence as if it were a well-constructed machine, each and all of whose parts are necessary for an external purpose, and are externally combined for that purpose; but not as an organic unity, whose parts are united by the one life that expresses itself in them all, and whose purpose is only that life itself. But to know the world is not an accidental or external purpose of the intelligence; it is the activity through which alone the intelligence can become conscious of itself—or, in other words, can exist as an intelligence at all. And the various categories or forms of thought by which it makes the world intelligible, are not external instruments it uses, but modes of its own activity, or stages in its own development. To complete the work of Kant, and clear it from these defects, philosophy must not only undertake the analysis of intelligence in relation to the intelligible world,—a work which, after all, leaves us "with the parts in our hands, but the informing spiritual unity awanting;" it must also retrace, with watchful consciousness, the unconscious synthetic process in which the intelligence first manifests its life, and through which it becomes possessor of itself and of its world; and it must show how each of the forms of that life has its reason and meaning in the one principle from which they spring. In so far as philosophy can succeed in this, it may meet scepticism with the further answer of a *solvitur ambulando;* for the rationality of the world is best proved by rationalising it. Still, it would be a mistake to think that reason's certitude of itself has to wait for this completed proof, or that there is no real answer to scepticism except omniscience. The primary answer of scepticism to itself—the answer which it gives by refuting itself—already is sufficient to show that reason can have to do only with itself; that all its conflicts and struggles are with itself, however they may seem to be with another; and that, therefore, there can never come into its life an antagonism which it has not in itself the means of reconciling. For reason, therefore, there can be no foreign object which it is impossible for it, in Kant's language, "to unite with its consciousness of itself," and no external necessity which it cannot make the means of its freedom or self-realisation.

To develop this idea, however, and to develop it in such a way as to give room for all the oppositions of thought and life, is something more than to feel it, rest in it, and enjoy it like a mystic. "The life of God—the life which the mind apprehends and enjoys as it rises to the absolute unity of all things—may be described as a play of love with itself; but this idea sinks to an edifying truism, or even to a platitude, when it does not embrace in it the earnestness, the pain, the patience, and labour, involved in the *negative* aspect of things." In other words, the intuitive apprehension of the absolute unity is nothing, unless that unity be brought into relation to the differences of the finite world; when it is asserted by itself it loses all its meaning. To the man of the world or the man of science, a religious or speculative optimism is apt to seem like a child's confidence in a world which he has never tried, rather than like that peace of spirit which has been confirmed by the completed experience of all its effort and pain. The words of triumph mean much or little, just in proportion to the greatness of the struggle, and the thoroughness with which it has been fought out, and they will not be listened to with patience on the lips of any one who has evaded his strongest enemies. The critical spirit is justly jealous of any solution which does not show, on the face of it, that the difficulty has been thoroughly sounded. Hence there is always a difficulty in producing a mutual understanding between those, on the one hand, whose minds are directed to the particular interests of life or to particular spheres of science, and those, on the other hand, who, either as poets, or religious men, or philosophers, live habitually in contemplation of the unity that is beyond all difference, the reconciliation that is above all conflict. By the conditions of their life, the former seem to be as naturally biassed toward a hard and unyielding dualism, which distrusts all "ideology,"—all harmonising and reconciling views of existence,—as the latter are prone to an easy idealism, which charms away the difficulties and reconciles the oppositions of life as if by a magic word. To bring about such an understanding, each of the two sides must be drawn out of itself, and brought into relation to each other. Now it is Hegel's effort, on the side of philosophy, so to overcome the abstractness of the speculative idea and develop its unity into difference, that he may force the scientific or practical consciousness, in its turn, to overcome its abstract and one-sided assertion of difference, and bring it into relation to the unity of thought. For if the unity of thought, the unity of the intelligence with itself, is to be found in all the intelligible universe,—in all the "subtlety of nature," and all the complex movement of history,—that unity must be more than the simple identity which philosophy has often found in it. If, as it was the aim or result of the Kantian philosophy to prove, self-consciousness is the principle of unity to which the world must be referred and by which it must be explained, self-consciousness must be a microcosm,—a world in itself, containing and resolving in the transparent simplicity or unity of its "glassy essence" all the differences and antagonisms which, in intensified form, it has to meet with in the macrocosm. The intelligence must not, therefore, be conceived as a mere resting identity, but rather as a complete process of differentiation and integration, which *rests* only in the sense that its movement returns upon itself. It will thus be, in Aristotle's language, an ἐνέργεια ἀκινησίας; in other words, it will be without movement or change, not because it is not active, but because its activity is determined only by itself. For only through such a concrete conception of the intelligence *in itself* will it be possible to understand how it should be able to reach *beyond itself*, and so to rise above the opposition of thought and things. Otherwise it must seem impossible that knowledge of the world should be attained, except by the absolute passivity of the intelligence; by the mind emptying itself of itself, and becoming a pure mirror, or a *tabula rasa* on which the external object may impress its image.

Now what is involved in the idea of self-consciousness? Kant, who first pointed out that the unity of the *ego* is presupposed in all our knowledge, has given a curious account of it. "Of the *ego*," he says, "one cannot even say that it is a conception of anything; it is rather a consciousness that accompanies all our conceptions. In this *I*, or *He*, or *It*—the thing which thinks—we have before us nothing but a transcendental subject of thought, an x or unknown quantity, which is known only through the thoughts which are its predicates, and of which, if we separate it from those thoughts, we cannot form the slightest conception. If we attempt to do so, we are obliged to revolve round it in a continual circle; for we cannot make any judgment about it without being obliged to presuppose and make use of the idea of it,—an inconvenience which is inevitable, because consciousness in itself is not, strictly speaking, the idea of a particular object, but a form for all ideas which deserve the name of knowledge—*i.e.*, for all ideas through which any object is thought." This remark of Kant's brings out the peculiarity of self-consciousness, that it is no simple unity or identity; for if so, it must be purely an object or purely a subject, but really it is both in one; all other things are *for it*, but it is *for itself*. This strikes Kant as "an inconvenience," which prevents us from knowing it as we may know other things,—as if the *ego* somehow, by reason of its duality as both *subject* and *object*, stood in its own light, and was guilty of a kind of circle-reasoning in pretending to know itself. But when we look at the matter more closely, it would seem that Kant is here himself guilty of a curious paralogism, in attacking what is our very highest type of knowledge, and rejecting it because it does not conform to his own preconceived ideas. It is as if one should say that it is impossible to see the sun because we cannot throw the rays of a candle upon it. But as it is the light which reveals both itself and the darkness, so it is self-consciousness through which we know both itself and all other things. If knowledge is the relation of an object to a conscious subject, it is the more complete, the more intimate the relation; and it becomes perfect when the duality becomes transparent, when subject and object are identified, and when the duality is seen to be simply the necessary expression of the unity,—in short, when consciousness passes into self-consciousness. "It is just the intelligence itself which Kant declares to be unintelligible." And the reason is, that Kant's mind was secretly possessed with the preconception that the one thing *entirely* intelligible is a pure abstract identity which has no division or difference in it all. This preconception, however, was shown by Kant himself to be a false one. It was his special work, in the 'Critique of Pure Reason,' to prove that every object of knowledge, as such, involves a relation to a subject; in other words, that it is *not* a simple identity, but involves difference, and unity in difference. But if so, then self-consciousness is the knowable *par excellence*, insomuch as in it the object, which is distinguished from the subject, is, at the same time, most perfectly coalescent with it. It was, in fact, just because Kant took pure identity as his ideal of knowledge, that he was driven to seek for absolute truth in a region beyond the objective consciousness, or, what to him was the same thing, beyond the phenomenal consciousness. And as such an identity is really unknowable and incomprehensible, he was obliged at the same time to confess that this region of pure self-identical subjectivity cannot be reached by knowledge, but only by faith. If, however, Kant's "reason" had thus to enter into the "intelligible world" or "kingdom of ends" "halt and maimed," it was because he had maimed it himself. It was his own definition of truth, or rather his tacit preconception of truth, which made truth unattainable to him, and which even made him reject its very quintessence and antitype in self-consciousness as unintelligible.

This failure of Kant, however, directly points to a new conception of knowledge, and a reform of logic. The old analytic logic was based on that very idea of identity by which Kant was misled. It started with the presupposition that each object is an isolated identity, itself and nothing more. It accepted the law of contradiction in a sense which involved a denial of the relativity or community of things. It separated object from subject, one thing from another; or, if it admitted relations between things, these were regarded by it as altogether external, or outside of the real nature of the things in themselves. But such a theory of knowledge is, as it were, broken in pieces against the idea of self-consciousness, in which the true unity, the pattern of all knowledge, is seen to be essentially complex or concrete,—a unity of differences, a circle of relations in itself. Self-consciousness is the standing enigma for those who would separate identity and difference; for it is not merely that, in one aspect of it, self-consciousness is a duality, and in another aspect a unity; duality and unity are so inseparably blended in it, that neither has any meaning without the other. Or, to put it still more definitely, the self exists as one self only as it opposes itself, as object, to itself, as subject, and immediately denies and transcends that opposition. Only because it is such a concrete unity, which has in itself a resolved contradiction, can the intelligence cope with all the manifoldness and division of the mighty universe, and hope to master its secrets. As the lightning sleeps in the dewdrop, so in the simple and transparent unity of self-consciousness there is held in equilibrium that vital antagonism of opposites, which, as the opposition of thought and things, of mind and matter, of spirit and nature, seems to rend the world asunder. The intelligence is able to understand the world, or, in other words, to break down the barrier between itself and things, and find itself in them, just because its own existence is implicitly the solution of all the division and conflict of things.

To see, however, that this is the case, and that in the intelligence, as the subject-object, there lies an adequate principle for the interpretation of nature and history, it is necessary that we should explain more fully what is involved in the idea of self-consciousness. For such an interpretation is possible only in so far as in self-consciousness are implicitly contained all the categories by which science and philosophy attempt to make the world intelligible,—a doctrine, the detailed proof of which is the object of the *Hegelian Logic*.

CHAPTER VIII.

THE HEGELIAN LOGIC.

WHEN we say that knowledge is possible, we imply that the intelligence can raise itself above the accidental, partial, changing point of view which belongs to the individual as such. If each man were forced to make himself the centre of the universe, and to regard things as important and real in proportion as they immediately affected his senses or were directly instrumental to the satisfaction of his wants, neither intellectual nor moral life could possibly be his. To make either attainable, he must be able to look at things *in ordine ad universum*—*i.e.*, he must be able to discount the influences of his immediate position and circumstances, even of his personal wishes and feelings, and to regard himself individually as one object among the other objects he knows. He must feel something of the same indifferent interest in himself, and apply something of the same impartial judgment to himself, which he feels and applies in relation to that which does not affect him at all,—to that which is distant in time and space from the immediate circle of his concerns. To live as a *moral* being, the individual must look at himself and treat himself from the point of view of the family, of the state, or of humanity, giving to his own desires and interests just the weight which they deserve when regarded from such higher centre, and *not* the exclusive weight which they claim when they are allowed to speak for themselves. The precept, that we should do to others as we would that they should do to us, has a practical value, not because in its literal sense it clearly marks out the path of duty,—for our wishes for another might be as unreasonable as our wishes for ourselves,—but because the effort to put ourselves sympathetically in another's place is generally the surest way of lifting us out of the close atmosphere of personal feelings. In like manner, *intellectual* life, the life of knowledge, is primarily an effort to break away from those things that are, as Aristotle says, "first for us,"—the immediate appearances and apprehensions of sense, which are different for each of us, and continually changing,—and to reach those things that are "first by nature"—the laws or principles which manifest themselves no more and no less in one set of appearances than another. To use an illustration of Kant, the confused Ptolemaic system is the one most natural to us: we would fain account for everything, in however complex and difficult a way, on the supposition that the universe revolves round our individual selves. But science and philosophy seek to introduce the Copernican system, with its simple and transparent order, by changing our point of view to the sun, the universal centre around which all things really revolve.

But *can* we thus really get out of ourselves? Can we free ourselves from the influence of our surroundings, and our very nature as individuals? Or, if we can do so to some extent, is there not a limit to the process in our very humanity? "Man never knows," says Goethe, "how anthropomorphic he is." If we can overleap the chasm that separates us from our fellow-men, can we expect also to get rid of the tendency, more or less definitely to humanise nature in the very act of taking knowledge of it? Or, even supposing that we can transcend all the divisions that separate finite things and beings from each other, is there not still an absolute gulf fixed between the finite and the infinite, which confines us to time and space, and hinders us from seeing things *sub specie æternitatis?*

This problem was one which already troubled Aristotle in the dawn of psychology. He solves it by the doctrine that the intelligence is not, strictly speaking, one thing or being to which you can assign separate qualities or attributes, and so distinguish it from other things and beings. It is, he declares, a universal capacity, and "has no other nature than this, that it is capable." It has "no foreign element" mingled with its pure universality, "which might confuse and interrupt its view of the object." Hence it is able "to master all objects—that is to say, to understand them." Translating these pregnant words into more modern terms, what they imply is, that the intelligence is not one thing among others in the intelligible world, but the principle in reference to which alone that world exists; and that, therefore, there is nothing in the nature of intelligence to prevent it from understanding a universe which is essentially the object of intelligence. The thinking subject, no doubt, is also an individual among other individuals; but, *as* a thinking subject, he is free of the world, emancipated from the limitations not only of his own individual being, but even of his generic nature. The individuality of a self-conscious being, as such, rests on a basis of universality; if he is conscious of himself in *opposition* to that which is not himself, he is at the same time conscious of self and not-self in *relation* to each other; and that implies that he is conscious of the unity that includes both. We may say, therefore, that he is not limited to himself; that just because he is a self, he transcends himself; that his life includes, in a higher sense, even that which it seems, in a lower sense, to exclude. Or, to approach more nearly to Aristotle's language, a self is not merely one thing or being, distinguished by certain qualities from other things or beings; rather he may be said to have all qualities or none; for he is capable of relating himself to all, and so making them parts of his own life: yet he is limited to none as a definite and final qualification of his own being. If he were, he could not be conscious of it as an object.

If this view be true, it follows that the intelligence of man, as it is implicitly universal, is capable of rising above, and abstracting from, all purely subjective associations, and seeing objects as they are in themselves, or, what is the same thing, from a universal point of view. This act of abstraction, in a more or less definite form, is implied in all man's existence, intellectual, moral, and even natural,—in so far as even in his simplest sensuous experience there is the latent working of a rational principle. But it is implied in a higher degree in science: for science is essentially the conscious and deliberate effort to break away from subjectivity, and see things as they objectively are. As such it involves a severe discipline of self-restraint, and even, we might say, a painful process of self-abnegation; for it is by no means an easy thing to thrust aside all our preconceptions and assumptions, or to allow them to be weighed in the scales of nature, without any attempt to bias the decision by which they may be found wanting. Yet in thus renouncing its subjective prepossessions, the mind is not renouncing itself. It is not, as Bacon seems to think, reducing itself to a passive mirror of an objective world. Rather it is thus making room for its own true activity, bringing itself into that central or universal attitude in which alone it can show what it is *as* mind. The activity of an intelligence is not pure till it has got rid of the accidental or particular element that clings to its immediate self, for then only can it rise to a new universal life, in which its movement is one with that of the object which it contemplates. For *it* is not, as Aristotle showed, like a thing which has special qualities, and which perishes when they are changed. *It* is not involved in the fate of the particular opinions and prepossessions which keep it from the knowledge of objects, but rather begins to energise freely and powerfully only when these have been cast aside.

Universality is readily confused with emptiness, because it is a freedom from all that is particular. And so a universal activity may easily be taken for passivity, because it is not the self-assertion of the subject of it against anything else. In this sense it is sometimes said that true science consists in silencing our own ideas that nature alone may speak. Nature, however, can speak only to an intelligence, and as an intelligence speaks in it. The aim of the negative discipline of science is to free the subjective intelligence from all that separates it from the object; but if by this process thought were really made passive and empty, along with the partiality and one-sidedness of consciousness, consciousness itself would disappear. The process of the liberation of thought from itself, therefore, is not the mere negation of thought,—which would necessarily be the negation of the object of thought also; it is the negation of thought and being alike *as separate from each other*, and the revelation of their implicit unity. Nor is this a pantheistic unity in which all distinction is lost; it is simply the unity of the intelligence with the intelligible world, which is presupposed in their difference, and in the light of which alone their difference can be truly understood. In abstracting from itself, as separate from and opposed to the object, in taking what is called a purely objective attitude, the intelligence has already implicitly shown that the object is not really a limit to it, or even something externally given to it. It could not take the point of view of the object if that point of view were not its own,—if in the object it met with something which was absolutely foreign to it. That it can thus, in its utmost self-surrender, still maintain itself,—that it can rise to a unity which is beyond its distinction *from* the object and its opposition *to* the object,—is already the pledge that all such opposition and distinction may be overcome and resolved; or, in other words, that the world may be shown to be not merely the object but also the manifestation of intelligence. When, therefore, the mind seems to have freed itself of all content of its own, it is just then that it begins to find *itself*—*i.e.*, to find the categories and forms of thought which constitute it —in the object. When it ceases to witness of itself, nature and history begin to witness of it. When it is silent, the "stones" begin to "cry out."

This doctrine, that we need only to cast aside all prepossessions, and take the world as it is, to find intelligence in it, is what Hegel attempts to prove in his 'Logic.' Commonly that 'Logic' is supposed to be the groundwork for something quite different,—for an attempt to construct nature *a priori*, and without reference to facts and experience. Now it is true that Hegel does there treat of the categories by which nature is made intelligible apart from the process of their application. This, however, is not because he is unaware that it is in the struggle to interpret experience that the intelligence is made conscious of its own forms. But he is of opinion that the categories must be considered in themselves and in their relation to each other,—rather than in relation to the objects to which they are applied or in which they are realised,—in order that it may be shown that there is law and order, unity in difference, in the mind as well as in the objects it knows. Hegel, in short, is, in his 'Logic,' simply seeking to prove that these different categories are not a collection of isolated ideas, which we find in our minds and of which we apply now one, now another, as we might try one after another of a bunch of keys upon a number of isolated locks; he is seeking to prove that the categories are not instruments which the mind *uses*, but elements in a whole, or the stages in a complex process, which in its unity the mind *is*. For the mind has no key but itself to apply to nature; in spelling out the meaning of things, it can only move through the circle of its own self-consciousness in relation to them. Its process is, therefore, a continuous process, with a beginning and end determined by the nature of self-consciousness itself. It is a *method*, and not merely an accidental succession of trials, that is needed to make the world scientifically intelligible, and in this method there is for the application of each category a time and place, which cannot be changed without confusion. Where, indeed, *shall* logical order be found, if it be not in the succession of the categories, on which all logical method is based? From the first judgment of perception in which it is asserted that a particular object *is*, to the last scientific and philosophic comprehension of that object in its relations to other things and to the mind that knows it, there is a necessary sequence which cannot be inverted or changed. And our thorough comprehension of the world must depend on the order and completeness with which this process of thought is followed out in reference to it. Now this movement it is for logic, as the science of method, to trace *in abstracto* from category to category up to the idea of self-consciousness, which is the category of categories, the organic unity of all the other categories. Thus logic will reach at once a definition of intelligence as the principle of unity in the world, and a complete idea of method, as the process by which that principle of unity is to be traced out and discovered in all the manifold diversities of things.

Why does Hegel begin with Being, and not, like Kant, with self-consciousness, if it be true that self-consciousness is the principle in which the explanation of all things is to be found? The answer to this question is implied in what has been already said. Hegel, no doubt, like Kant, holds that a relation to self-consciousness is implied in the first apprehension of an object, and that Being or Existence is essentially Being or existence *for a self*. But this relation of all existence, as object, to a conscious subject, is, in the first instance, implicit. In asserting that an object *is*, we do not assert that it is essentially related to other objects or to the intelligence. On the contrary, in our first way of looking at things, each object seems to be isolated from all the rest, as well as from the mind that knows it. The common consciousness at first seems to view the world as if it were a mere collection of things, one beside another, and a succession of events, one after another, without any vital or essential connection; nor does it regard the mind, to which these things and events are present, as related to them in any less external way than that in which they are related to each other. And though it might be shown that even in the external relation of things as in one space and time, a more essential connection of them to each other and to thought is presupposed, yet such connection, just because it is *presupposed* in the common consciousness, is not present to it. For it, therefore, each thing stands by itself, without any but an accidental connection with anything else. Thus the common consciousness lives in abstraction, though it has never abstracted. It has never, indeed, needed to abstract, just because it has never been conscious, or at least never been clearly conscious, of the whole to which belong the different objects and elements which it isolates. Nor does science at first correct this isolating tendency of common thought; rather it seeks in its first movement to exaggerate that tendency, and press it to the utmost point of abstraction. For the first accidental connection of things in the experience of the individual must be seen to *be* accidental, and the first subjective associations produced by such experience in the individual mind must be broken, ere the true relativity and connection of objects can be known. This is the meaning of the scientific discipline of which we have been speaking, — the discipline by which the mind, in Baconian phrase, is taught to renounce its "idols." The ordinary experimental methods destroy such false associations by what is really a practical development of the process of abstraction — *i.e.*, by isolating the object or quality in question from the others with which it has been accidentally united.

Thus, then, the method of exclusion, negation, abstraction, in which an object is fixed by itself, and isolated from all its usual surroundings, has its place and value as the first step in scientific investigation. But that method may easily be misinterpreted, and made the basis of a false theory, if it be considered by itself; for then it will give rise to the doctrine that what a thing is, it is *in itself*, apart from all relation to other things or the mind. Such a doctrine is easily accepted by common-sense, for it is only its own isolating external way of thinking, brought to a clearer consciousness of itself. But, grasped by the understanding, and logically worked out to its consequences, it leads directly to the conclusion that the reality of things,—that which things are *in themselves*,—is unknown and unknowable. For all

Objective Dialectic.

existence is but the manifestation, and all knowledge but the apprehension, of relations; and the attempt to strip a thing of its relations must therefore end in reducing it to a *caput mortuum* of abstraction of which nothing can be said. The real meaning of the scientific abstraction is thus perverted: for science sets a thing by itself, not that it may find out what it is apart from all relations, but that it may disclose its *immanent* or native relativity. It rejects all accidental and extraneous associations that may force its object to reveal its own intelligible nature—*i.e.*, its essential relation to other things and to the mind. Now Hegel only applies this same method to the forms of thought implied in all existence. He takes the categories, the ideas of Being, Existence, Cause, &c., each by itself, not in order to divorce each of these thoughts from all other thoughts, and from the mind which they constitute, but rather for the opposite reason,—in order to prove that they cannot be so divorced. In other words, his object is to show in relation to each of the categories that it is not merely *capable* of being associated or combined with the others, but that it has an immanent relativity or necessary connection with them, so that the other categories spring out of it the moment we attempt to confine it to itself. All subjective associations being destroyed, the pure objective association, the connection of idea with idea, which arises from, or, more strictly speaking, *is* their own nature, will necessarily show itself. As the elasticity of the spring manifests itself only the more evidently, the more firmly it is pressed home to itself, so the more decisively a thought is fixed by abstraction in its isolated definiteness, the more clear it becomes that it has, or rather is, a relativity,—*i.e.*, that it has other thoughts implicit in itself. Ideas are not dead things, but "have hands and feet." And the way in which such relativity springs out of a category, just when it is fixed to itself and isolated from all other categories, has already been indicated in what has been said of the "thing in itself." Isolate a thing from all its relations, and try to assert it by itself; at once you find that you have negated it, as well as its relations. The thing in itself is nothing. The absolute or pure affirmation,—just because it is absolute or pure,—is its own negation. Referred to itself and itself only, it ceases to be itself; for its definition, that which made it itself, was its relation to that which was not itself. Thus we come upon the apparent paradox, that opposites are distinguished only when they are related, and that, if we carry the opposition to the point in which the relation ceases, the distinction ceases at the same time. And this leads us to the further result, that the relation to its opposite or negative is the one essential relation out of which a thought cannot be forced,—the relation which maintains itself when all extraneous associations are swept away. A thought is essentially the relation or the movement towards its opposite or negative; and this is proved by the fact that if it be absolutely isolated from that opposite, it immediately becomes indistinguishable from it. Its connection with its opposite is, therefore, the first link in the chain of essential relativity that connects it with the whole body of other thoughts and with the intelligence.

"Being and not-Being are identical." This mysterious utterance of Hegel, round which so much controversy has waged, and which has seemed to many but a caprice of metaphysic run mad, may now be seen to have a serious meaning. It does not mean that Being and not-Being are not also distinguished; but it does mean that the distinction is not absolute, and that if it is made absolute, at that very moment it disappears. The whole truth, therefore, cannot be expressed either by the simple statement that Being and not-Being are identical, or by the simple statement that they are different. But the consideration of what these abstractions are in themselves when we isolate them from each other,—just as a scientific man might isolate a special element in order to find the essential relativity or energy that lies in it,—shows that their truth is not *either* their identity *or* their difference, but is their *identity in difference.* But one who has apprehended this thought has already risen above the abstractions whose unity in difference he has seen. He is like the scientific man who has discovered an identity of principle connecting phenomena between which formerly he had seen no essential relation. By such discovery the mere external view of them as different things, related only by adjacent place or time, has disappeared, and the one phenomenon has become the counterpart or complementary aspect of the other. In like manner, the thinker who has fully seen into the correlativity of given opposites has reached a new attitude of thought in regard to them. They have become for him inseparable elements of a higher unity, which is now seen to be organic or vital. Or the whole thought is seen to be a process through certain phases, each of which necessitated the other, and by the unity of which it—the whole thought—is constituted. Nor does the movement stop here. The whole thought reached in this way has again its opposite or negative, which it at once excludes and involves, and the process may be repeated in regard to it, with the result of reaching a still higher unity, a more complex thought, in which it and its opposite are elements. And so on, through ever-widening sweep of differentiation and integration, till the whole body of thought is seen in its organic unity and development,—every fibre of it alive with relation to the whole in which it is a constituent element.

Has the process which has just been described a natural beginning and end? If it be true that self-consciousness includes or involves in it all the categories, it is obvious that the end is in the full *definition* of self-consciousness—*i.e.*, the full analysis or differentiation of all the contents of the idea of self-consciousness, and their integration in that idea, as the unity of them all. And, on the other hand, its beginning must obviously be in the simplest and most abstract category, —which, as we have seen, is the category of Being,— the category by which a thing is referred to itself, *as if* it had no relation to other things or to the mind. And the process which connects the beginning with the end is just the gradual revelation of these two relativities,—to things and to the mind,—which are implicit or presupposed, but not explicit or consciously present, in our first immediate attitude of thought. The *first* main division of logic, then, will have to do with the categories in which, as yet, relativity is not expressed; categories like Being, Quality, Quantity, which, though they involve, do not immediately suggest, any relation of the object to which they are applied to any other object. The *second* main division will have to do with categories such as Essence and Existence, Force and Expression, Substance and Accident, Cause and Effect, which force us to go beyond the object with which we are dealing, and to connect it with other objects, or at least with something that is not immediately presented to us in the perception of it. And the *last* main division will have to do with categories, such as those of final cause and organic unity, by which the object is characterised as related to intelligence, or as having in it that self-determined nature of which the intelligence is the highest type; or to put it otherwise, it will have to do with categories by which the object is determined as essentially being, or having in it, an ideal unity which is reached and realised in and through all the manifoldness of its existence. The general argument of the 'Logic,' when we pursue it through all these stages, therefore is this: that reality,—which at first is present to us as the Being of things which are regarded as standing each by itself, determined in quality and quantity, but as having no necessary relations to each other,—comes in the process of thought to be known as an endless aggregate of essentially related and transitory existences, each of which exists only as it determines and is determined by the others, according to universal laws,—and finally, is discovered to lie in a world of objects, each and all of which exist only in so far as they exist for intelligence, and in so far as intelligence is revealed or realised in them. And that this, indeed, is the movement of thought by which the reality of things is disclosed, is proved by the demonstration that the categories of *Being*,—used in the first attitude of thought, which corresponds to our simplest and most unsophisticated consciousness of things,—when fully understood and reasoned out, necessarily lead us to the categories of Relation, employed in the second attitude of thought, which corresponds generally to the scientific or reflective consciousness; and that these in turn, when fully comprehended and pressed to their consequences, necessarily pass into the categories of *Ideal Unity*, or, as it is sometimes expressed, "the notion,"—categories used in the third stage of consciousness, which corresponds to philosophy. Science is the *truth* of common-sense, because the points of view from which the former considers the world, include and transcend the points of view from which it is regarded by the latter; and philosophy is the *truth* of science for the same reason, because it is science and something more. This something more, however, in each case is not merely something externally added to what went before; it is a vital growth from it,—a transformation which takes place in it, by reason of latent forces that are already present. In this way self-consciousness—the last category or point of view—is seen to sum up and interpret all that went before; for while, like our first immediate consciousness of things, it is a direct assertion of independent Being—and while, like reflection, it includes difference and relation,—it goes beyond both in so far as it expresses the integration of differences — a relation of elements which, though opposed, are yet identified.

To attempt to prove these points in detail would be to work out again the whole process of the Hegelian Logic. The general account of it just given may, however, be made a little more distinct, if we consider more closely the process of knowledge as it advances through science to philosophy. It is obvious that the beginning of knowledge lies in taking things by themselves, as they lie before us in perception; in excluding all preconceptions, and accurately observing their qualities, and determining the quantity of each quality. Such observation is the first indispensable basis of science; but it can hardly yet itself be called science. It deserves the name, if at all, only where the observer, in his selection of facts to observe and his determination of their relative importance, is really guided by ideas of relation of which he is not definitely conscious; for scientific genius shows itself first in a kind of "instinct of reason," which anticipatively apprehends the fruitful direction for observation and experiment. But the pure observer soon finds that the qualities and quantities with which he deals are continually changing, and that the intelligence cannot find in them the fixed object which it seeks, unless it is able to go beyond them or beneath them to something that cannot be observed. Such a deeper reality, such a principle of permanence in change, is already suggested to him by the fact that he does not find the quality and quantity of things to change altogether irrespectively of each other, but to be linked together in a certain mutual dependence, so that, with a little more or a little less of the same element, the quality of a thing is suddenly altered. But this, as a mere fact, is not any longer sufficient for him, when he has come to apprehend that change of quality is not an accidental or partial phenomenon, but that every quality as it exists is in process of changing. Thus the final experience of that mode of thought, which fixes each finite thing to itself and takes it to be only what it is *in itself*, is that such things can quite as truly be said "not to be" as "to be." Their being is a "becoming" or change. Unless, therefore, we can get beyond this continual flux of unsubstantial things, this endless change of phenomena, the intelligence is denuded of its objects, and falls back upon itself in scepticism. This, in fact, is the first natural effect of the growing consciousness that appearances—things as they are immediately present to us for observation—are essentially inconstant and fluctuating; for by this experience all that common-sense held to be reality is discerned to be unreal, and as yet nothing else had disclosed itself to take the place of that which has disappeared. In this scepticism, however, science is born;—science, of which the essential characteristic is to recognise that things are not as they seem, but that beyond and through the seeming we can apprehend that which really is, the one force through the manifold expression, the abiding law through the fleeting phenomena. The scientific or reflective consciousness, therefore, may be said to begin with the negation of the immediate reality of finite things, and to aim at finding some deeper ground or principle in reference to which they may be conceived to have a kind of secondary or *mediated* reality.

This scientific consciousness has, however, a certain growth or development within itself by which its first antagonistic or dualistic mode of thought is gradually transcended and transmuted. And as in the first stage of thought, which began with purely affirmative determination of things,—as if they existed in themselves, independent of all relation,—there was a continual progress toward the recognition of the negative or relative aspect of them, the aspect in which they are seen to be essentially finite and transitory; so in this second stage, which begins with the absolute contrast of real and apparent, substance and accident, there is a continual progress toward an ever clearer apprehension of the essential connection of these two opposite aspects of things, and finally, to the discerning of the unity that binds them to each other. At first, as is natural, the opposition is stated most strongly,— so strongly that it seems to involve a denial of all relations whatever; as when, in the early Eleatic school, the "one" was abstractly opposed to the "many," which was regarded as purely apparent and unreal. But it was soon recognised that, by this absolute separation, both terms are deprived of their meaning. If the many, the changing, the phenomenal, is unreal in the sense that it contains its negative in itself, equally unreal is the one, the permanent, the substance, which is abstractly opposed to these, and which is, in fact, nothing but that negative positively expressed. Plato, and still more Aristotle, found that what was wanted was not "the one *beyond* the many" merely, but "the one *in* the many." And the progress of science up to the present day has been a continuous advance towards the reconciliation of the two terms in a conception of the inner reality or principle of things, which should make that reality or principle the complete explanation, and nothing but the explanation, of their external appearances and changing phenomena. Looking at this progressive movement of the scientific consciousness, we can understand how it is that modern science, though it has not itself got beyond the dualism of phenomenal and real, yet takes up so marked an attitude of antagonism to the more decided dualism of earlier days, and is prone to denounce as "metaphysical" what is really just an initial stage of its own mode of thought. Thus, for example, Comte condemns the reference of phenomena to "forces" and "substances," which are, he maintains, either pure negations or the abstract repetitions of the phenomena they are adduced to explain. Science, in his view, should confine itself to the investigation of the "laws" of the resemblance, coexistence, and succession of phenomena, these laws being regarded simply as the generalised restatement of the phenomena themselves. In thus speaking, however, Comte is really admitting what he seems to deny. Such "generalised restatement" is obviously something more than a simple reaffirmation of the phenomena themselves. A law is at once the negation and the reaffirmation of the phenomena that fall under it: it is contrasted with them, as permanent with changing, as unity with multiplicity, and yet it is one with them, as the principle by reference to which alone they are lifted above mere appearances, or illusions of the moment. The defect, however, of this whole scientific mode of thought is that, while it goes beyond the immediate phenomena to seek for an explanation of them, it is never able to find a complete explanation. For the principle, to which the phenomena are thus referred, never exhausts their meaning, but rather itself presupposes those very phenomena. In other words, the law, which is supposed to explain the phenomena, though necessarily distinguished from

Defects of Scientific Thought.

them, is essentially related to them, and, in its turn, looks for explanation to them. This double aspect of the idea of law sometimes leads writers who are not clearly conscious of their own categories into a curious inconsistency of statement. For, while at one time they tell us that the law is *merely* the generalised expression of the phenomena,—as if their translation into the form of law were something indifferent and unnecessary,—at another time they declare with equal emphasis that we know the phenomena *only* when we know their laws, as if the law were *not* merely a generalised repetition of the phenomena, but the central principle, in reference to which alone the true value and significance of the phenomena can be known.

The key to the difficulty, however, is found when it is seen that the scientific mode of thought, though necessary as a stage of knowledge, has an essential imperfection clinging to it, which can be corrected only by going beyond it to the philosophical mode of thought, or what Hegel calls the *Begriff*. In scientific reflection we have always two terms which are essentially related, and in one of which the explanation of the other is sought. Yet, just because of this essential relation, the explanation can never be complete. The categories used are such as substance and accident, force and expression, inner and outer being, cause and effect. In each of these cases we have an essential relation of two terms of such a kind that, though the explanation of the second term is always sought in the first, yet the first term has no significance except in relation to the second. We have, therefore, in employing such categories, necessarily involved ourselves in a self-contradiction,—the self-contradiction of explaining everything by a term, which yet is essentially relative to that which is to be explained. Thus we explain the accidents by referring them to the substance; but the substance has no meaning apart from the accidents. Nor does it make any difference if, instead of such a reciprocity of terms, we have a series, as when we say that the cause explains the effect, but is itself to be explained by the effect of another cause; for this further need of explanation simply means that the cause does not *fully* explain its effect. Its difference from the effect, and its essential relation to it, is the very reason that forces us to seek explanation of it in another cause. We have therefore, in this and every similar movement of thought, a contradiction which needs to be solved: for that which is set up in opposition to the relative as absolute, and, indeed, as *its* absolute, is yet itself correlative with it, and so again must be recognised as *not* being absolute. Those who deal in such categories, therefore, fall into a kind of fluctuation or alternation of language, of which the above-mentioned uncertainty in regard to law is one instance. Nor is this fluctuation a mere accident. The category that rules their thoughts forces them to contradict themselves, as it turns first one and then the other of its sides to the light. For the most part, however, they do not bring together the different aspects of their thought, and hence they do not feel the difficulty, or the need of solving it by a higher category. Often, indeed, this unconsciousness may be an advantage in a work, which requires rather the thorough and unhesitating application of a category than the perception of its limits. For, as the higher categories have their full value, only when they come as the solution of difficulties which arise out of the lower categories, so the philosophical explanation of things, by means of the former, can only be legitimately arrived at as the last reinterpretation of the scientific explanation of them by means of the latter. But, on the other hand, the unresolved dualism, which is left by the application of the scientific categories, shows the necessity of a reinterpretation of the results of science by other higher categories, as it also shows that this reinterpretation—which constitutes the peculiar work of philosophy—is no mere useless or extraneous addition to science, but a necessary development of it. Comte, indeed, as we have seen, has an easier method of dealing with the difficulty, by simply denying altogether the distinction between real and phenomenal, between fact and law, which gives rise to it. But this, if it were taken as meaning what it expresses, would be no true solution of the problem, but simply a recurrence to that first sensuous consciousness for which the opposition of seeming and reality did not exist,—a consciousness which must be disturbed and overthrown, ere even the dawn of science is possible. For the doubt and wonder in which science arises, is the doubt and wonder that things are not what they seem; and if it is possible again to find the reality in the seeming, it must be by a reconciliation of those opposites, and not simply by obliterating the opposition.

Where, then, are we to find such a complete reconciliation? The highest conception of the world which science presents to us is the conception of a multiplicity of substances, acting and reacting on each other, and by their action and reaction producing continual changes in each other according to unchanging laws. Each substance, thus, by the condition of its being, stands in relation to that which is opposed to it, and which gives rise to changes in it; yet each maintains itself *in* change, in so far as it changes according to a law—*i.e.*, it has a definite relation to the other substance, which manifests itself in its change. In this way of looking at things, however, there is a certain ambiguity and inconsistency. For, while we start with the idea of isolated substances which have an existence of their own, and which change only because they are brought into relation to each other, it appears as we go on that what maintains itself is the law of the relation itself, apart from which the substances have no existence whatever. Substantiality and Relativity are thus seen to be not two ideas, but one, and the truth is to be found not in either separately but in their union; which means that nothing can be said to be substantial in the sense of having an existence independent of relation, but only in the sense of including its relativity in its own being. In other words, nothing is substantial except in so far as it is a subject or self which maintains itself in change, because its change is determined by its own nature, and is indeed only the necessary manifestation of that nature. To speak of different substances, which yet have *no* independent nature apart from their action and reaction on each other, is a manifest contradiction; for the necessity to which, according to this view, the different substances are supposed to be subjected, is itself the only true substance. Or what we really have before us in such a reciprocity is not a duality of things externally related, but a unity which expresses itself and maintains itself in duality. The real substance has to be sought for, not in the two things taken separately, but in the principle which divides, and at the same time unites, them. Determination by another is thus always ultimately to be explained as self-determination, though we may have to seek the self in question somewhere else than in the things which were at first taken to be substantial, but which may turn out to be mere "moments" or elements in some higher existence. This is what Hegel means by saying that the "truth of necessity is freedom." Necessity exists for any thing or being only in so far as it is determined by another,—and if it has no life or movement of its own which is not so determined, *it* in itself has no reality whatever that should make us regard it as an individual thing or substance at all: *it* is but one side or phase of the existence of something else, which is not determined by another, but by itself. The ultimate reality of things, therefore, which the common consciousness seeks in their purely unrelated or independent being, and which science seeks in their existence as essentially related to each other, is only to be found in what we may call their ideal character, as unities of correlative differences, or unities which manifest themselves in difference yet in this difference are still one with themselves. Thus that alone can truly be called a reality which maintains and realises itself in a process of differentiation and reintegration of differences. "Nothing really exists which is not *determined* and *relative*,—nothing which is not in a process of becoming or change." This was proved by the *first* stage of the 'Logic,' which carried us from the immediate consciousness of things to science. "Nothing really exists which is not *self-determined* and *self-related*,—which has not a self which it maintains through all its changes." This is proved by the *second* stage of the 'Logic,' which carries us from the first scientific consciousness of the opposition of appearances and reality, to the perception that the real manifests itself in the appearance and its change: or, what is the same thing, the perception that what we call the *real* is fundamentally ideal. For, whereas to the reflective consciousness the ideal seems to be an abstract law or principle, which is different from the facts, or represents only one side of the facts, through which we apprehend it, it is now seen that this ideal unity is the fact of facts, the principle from which they all spring, and to which they return. Reality lies,—not, as common-sense supposes, in the mere individual taken by itself—nor, as science seems to teach, in the mere particular which is related to other particulars; it lies in the relation, or principle of relation, itself,—in the universal which differentiates or particularises itself and yet is one with itself in its particularity. Or, to express all in a word, " the real is the rational or intelligible; " *i.e.*, it is that which is capable of being thoroughly understood by the intelligence, just because it has in it the essential nature of the intelligence or self-consciousness, as a unity which is one with itself, not by the absence of difference, but rather by means of the difference, which it at once asserts and overcomes.

The idea which we are now examining may be illustrated by the Leibnitzian conception of the world as a universe of monads, each of which is itself a world. Each monad or real substance, on this view, is a microcosm, which *ideally*, or in its *perceptions*, takes the whole life of the world into itself, and yet, in spite of all this ideal relativity, is not *really* determined by anything but itself. Each is thus in itself a reflection of the whole, while yet it remains a complete whole in itself, developing entirely for itself in absolute freedom through all the changes of its purely inward life, though these changes correspond exactly to the outward movements of the great world without it. In this way, by the distinction of the *real* and *ideal* aspects of the monad, Leibnitz thinks to avoid the difficulty of combining in it the opposite conceptions of relativity and independent being, — universality and individuality, necessity or determination by others and freedom or determination by itself. This distinction is, however, really an evasion of the difficulty, and Leibnitz himself is obliged to give it up in relation to God, the monad of monads,—in whom, as the absolute unity of ideality and reality, he finds the ground of the harmony between the perceptions of each monad and the existence of the rest, and the reason why, notwithstanding their independence, they form parts of one world. Thus, though in relation to each other these monads may be free, in relation to God they have no freedom or self-determination whatever.

At this point, however, we come upon a great difficulty which arises in connection with the conception of reality which has just been presented. So soon as we are driven to recognise that reality can be found in that and that only which has a principle of self-determination in itself, we seem forced to recognise that the only reality is God. Though, therefore, the necessity of nature may have been shown to be freedom, yet it would seem that there is room for only one freedom in the world, the freedom of the absolute Being, which reduces all other things and beings to his mere determinations or the modes of his attributes; and the only other alternative to this would seem to be a monadism which isolates each substance from all the others, and absolutely confines it to itself, and which leaves room neither for ideal nor for real relations between it and anything else. In order to escape from this dilemma we would require what at first must seem to be an absolute contradiction—viz., such an idea of the absolute unity to which we are obliged to refer all existence, as should yet leave room for a real freedom and independence, a real self-centred life, in other beings than itself. And if such a conception is impossible, we do not seem to have gained much more by referring all things to an absolute subject, than if we had referred them merely to an absolute substance.

Now it is the main work of the *third* part of the 'Logic' to develop such an idea out of the simple conception of the monad or self-determining principle, which was the result reached by the *second* part of it. Here, as in the other cases, we must confine ourselves to indicating the general thought which runs through this development. The key to the difficulty was partly seen by Leibnitz himself, when he pointed out that a true organism is a unity of organisms, organic in all its parts. The life of the body is not a principle that dominates over dead members, and uses them as instruments to realise itself; it is *in* all the members, so that each of them in turn may be regarded as means and end to the others. There is, no doubt, a unity of the whole that subordinates all the parts, but it only subordinates them, so to speak, by surrendering or imparting itself to them, and giving to them a certain independent life,—a life which, though embraced in a wider circle, is still centred in itself. Now a *self*-determining principle, as such, is necessarily of this sort; it is not like a law which is imposed upon a foreign matter, for its only matter is itself. In determining, it determines *itself;* in producing differences, it produces *itself in them.* Its assertion or manifestation of itself is, therefore, in a sense, a denying of itself, a giving of itself away. Its life is a dying to live. It is true that we must add that this negation of itself can never be absolute. In the differences and opposition the unity must be maintained. The independence of the separate organs in the body must not be such as to break their connection with each other, and with the unity of the whole. But this connection is maintained, not by an external subordination, but by the completeness with which the life of the whole is communicated to the parts, so that, to realise themselves, they must become subservient to it. In like manner a world in which the central principle is a self-determining Being, while, in one aspect of it, it seems to be a unity in which no room is left for difference, in another aspect of it breaks into an infinite number of fragments, each of which seems to be centred in itself. It is not like the universe of Spinoza, in which every difference of mind is lost in the abstract attribute of infinite intelligence, and every distinction of matter in the abstract attribute of infinite extension; it is a universe in which "every thought is a truth, and every particle of dust an organisation;" a macrocosm made up of microcosms, which is all in every part.

> "Flower in the crannied wall,
> I pluck you out of the crannies;—
> Hold you here, root and all, in my hand,
> Little flower,—but if I could understand
> What you are, root and all, and all in all,
> I should know what God and man is."

Under such a conception the usual antithesis of individualism and pantheism fails us, and our idea of the world seems to involve both at once, or to fall into a kind of alternation between them, such as is found in the monadism of Leibnitz, or in the later theory of Schelling, in which all the differences of things were said to be " not qualitative but merely quantitative,"—*i.e.*, to be differences that from the highest point of view might be neglected as unessential. This, however, were to forget that though the organism is organic in all its parts, yet these parts have their specific determination, and that it is through this specific determination that they form one whole. It were to forget that though a self-determining principle necessarily is present in its determinations, and gives them thus a certain independence, yet that they in turn are limited in themselves, and only maintain themselves as the principle realises itself in them; or, in other words, as they in turn surrender themselves to the life of the whole. Their capacity of so surrendering themselves, in short, is the measure of their reality. Thus the unity as a self-determining principle is *in* the differences, but it is also in their negation, by which they pass beyond themselves as individuals and so return into the unity.

" The reality is the universal, which goes out of itself, particularises itself, opposes itself to itself, that it may

Idea of Organic Unity.

reach the deepest and most comprehensive unity with itself." Such expressions seem to be breaking through the very limits of language, by continual self-contradiction; yet they only distinctly analyse a thought which we continually use without analysis when we speak of a self, of self-consciousness or of self-determination. And as it has been shown that the "truth of necessity is freedom," we are compelled by the very development of the scientific conception of law to recognise that the ultimate interpretation of things must be in harmony with this idea. This, as we have seen, is equivalent to saying that the world is an organic unity. By the organic unity of the world, however, it is not meant merely that the world as a whole is to be interpreted on the *analogy* of the living body, or of a plant or animal. Such an organism only imperfectly realises the idea of which we are speaking; and if the world were organic in this fashion, it would not be a self-determined whole, in which all differences were brought back to unity. Or, even if we suppose all the differences of the world as an objective system could be brought to unity by means of such an idea, the thought or consciousness for which it exists would be left out; for the animal, though an organic unity, is not such a unity *for itself*. It probably never rises above the stage of feeling, in which the self is not yet clearly distinguished from, and related to, the world without. The supreme difference of subject and object is wanting to, or imperfectly expressed in, its life, and therefore there is not in it the possibility of the supreme reconciliation of intelligence with itself. If, therefore, the conception of an ideal or self-determining principle, with which we begin this third stage of the Logic, be fully developed, it will be seen to find its final form and expression only in *self-consciousness*, as the unity in difference of subject and object, self and not-self; for here only have we an ideal principle which is conscious of itself, and, consequently, complete in itself; here only have we a principle which develops to the utmost difference and opposition against itself, and yet returns into transparent unity with itself.

This may be seen more clearly if we consider what the life of self-consciousness is. In the first place, self-consciousness presupposes consciousness — *i.e.*, it is a consciousness of self in opposition, yet in relation, to a not-self. Yet in this distinction a higher unity is presupposed; for the self can be conscious of itself as so distinguished and related, only in so far as it overreaches the distinction between itself and its object. Thus beneath the conscious duality of self and not-self there is an unconscious unity, which reveals itself in the fact that the whole life of an intelligence is an effort to overcome its own dualism,—in *knowledge* to find itself, in *action* to realise itself, in an object or a world of objects, which at first presents itself as a stranger and even an enemy. For, as we have seen in our review of the previous stages of the 'Logic,' the world for the immediate consciousness of man is merely a world of things unrelated even to each other; and even when science so far overcomes this first consciousness, so as to discover law or relation in them, yet this relativity is not yet unity, not yet the pure transparent identity-in-difference of self-consciousness. Hence the intelligence cannot yet find itself in the object, or, what is the same thing, cannot see the essential relation of the object to

The Absolute Idea.

itself. When, however, we become conscious that the truth of necessity is freedom, or, in other words, that the reality of things is to be found in the ideal unity or self-determining principle realised in them,—the mask of strangeness is taken from the face of nature, and we begin to find in *it* the same spiritual principle which we are conscious of in ourselves. The world, however it may seem to oppose, is really the field for the realisation of intelligence; if it seems to resist us, it is because we are not yet at one with ourselves. For "all things must work together" for him whose nature is reason, and whose activity is only to realise himself as reason—*i.e.*, to realise the spiritual principle, which is at the same time his own nature and the nature of things. The whole theoretical and practical movement of self-consciousness thus culminates in what Hegel calls "the absolute idea" —*i.e.*, in the idea of a self-consciousness which manifests itself in the difference of self and not-self, that through this difference, and by overcoming it, it may attain the highest unity with itself. This, the last category, contains and implies all the other categories; and, in another way, it has been shown to be implied in each and all of them. For what the whole 'Logic' has proved is, that if we take the categories seriously, abstracting from all subjective associations, and fixing our attention on their objective dialectic,—or, in other words, if we leave the categories to define themselves by the necessary movement of thought through which they carry us,— they lead us in the end to this idea of self-consciousness as their ultimate meaning or truth.

From the above sketch of the 'Logic,' which is necessarily somewhat summary and therefore external, it may at least be seen what is the general character of the task which Hegel proposed to himself. It was nothing but the completion of that work which had been begun by Plato in the 'Parmenides' and the 'Sophist,' and which had first reached something like a systematic form in the 'Metaphysic' of Aristotle. For it was Plato who first separated the categories from their concrete application, and tried to follow out for itself the dialectic which belongs to them when thus taken as independent objects. And it was Aristotle who first tried to gather these first principles of Being and Knowing into a systematic whole, culminating in the idea of the absolute reality, or of God as the "absolute self-consciousness" ($\nu o \eta \sigma \iota s\ \nu o \eta \sigma \epsilon \omega s$). Hegel came back to the task with all the advantages of the modern development of science, by which the categories of reflection had been brought into clear consciousness, and shown to contain the keys to the secrets of nature. He came back to it after Kant had proved that the categories are only forms of expression for the unity of self-consciousness in relation to the world of objects. What remained for him, therefore, was to show that these categories are simply the necessary differentiation of the unity of intelligence; or, what is the same thing, that the idea of self-consciousness is the complete integration of them all. So far as he was successful in this, the result of his work was to overcome the dualism, which Aristotle had still left, between the pure intelligence and the intelligible world which is its object. For if, as Kant had shown, objects exist only for the conscious self and through application of the categories, and if all these categories, from the simplest conception of Being up to the most complex idea of causality and final causality, are but elements or moments of a truth which is completely stated only in the idea of self-consciousness, it follows that the objective world is and can be nothing but the manifestation of intelligence, or the means whereby it attains the fullest realisation of itself. Thus it is proved that there is a *spiritual* principle of unity,—a principle of unity which is renewed in every conscious self,— underlying all the antagonisms of the world, even its apparent antagonism to spirit itself. For such a self, therefore, there can be no absolute limit, or irreconcilable division, within or without. The native faith of the intelligence in itself has been justified by a thorough discussion and exhaustion of all the sources of scepticism. In spite of the apparent contingency or external necessity by which things seem to be ruled, it has been shown that "that only is real which is rational;" and in spite of the resistance which things present to what seem to be our highest aims and endeavours, it has been shown that "that only is rational which is real."

CHAPTER IX.

THE APPLICATION OR DEVELOPMENT OF THE LOGICAL IDEA — RELATION OF THE HEGELIAN PRINCIPLE TO CHRISTIANITY.

THE account of the Hegelian Logic given in the last chapter may serve as at least a partial answer to some of the ordinary objections made to it,—objections based upon the absoluteness of distinctions to which it attaches only a subordinate importance. The Hegelian Logic is at once a Logic and a Metaphysic—*i.e.*, it treats at once of the method and of the matter of knowledge, of the processes by which truth is discovered, and of the truth itself in its most universal aspects. In Hegel's view there is no merely formal process of intelligence—no process of intelligence which is not also a determination of its object by categories;—and the advance from less to more perfect knowledge is a continual transition from one category to another by which that determination is changed, and made more complete and accurate. While, therefore, knowledge is a process which, in its first aspect, seems to involve the negation of intellectual activity, and the absolute surrender of the mind to an indifferent and external object, it is really a process in which the mind is continually bringing that object more and more within the net of its categories, and changing its aspect, till all its strangeness has disappeared, and it has been made one with the thought that apprehends it. Thus the investigation of the object turns out to be at the same time the evolution of the mind in relation to it; and the highest category by which *it* is determined is at the same time the discovery of its essential relativity to the mind for which it is, and the recognition that in thus dealing with an object, the mind is really dealing with itself—or in other words, with something that forms an essential element in its consciousness of self. Thus the perfect revelation of what the object is, is also the return of intelligence into itself, or rather the discovery that in all its travels, it has never really gone beyond itself. The highest fruit of knowledge is the deepening of self-consciousness.

We may illustrate this view by reference to the ordinary opposition of *a priori* and *a posteriori*. According to Leibnitz, all knowledge was developed from within, however it might appear to come from without; for the monad evolved all its ideas and perceptions from itself by a pure *a priori* process. To Locke, on the other hand, or at least to many of the school of Locke, knowledge was a filling of the mind with experience from without, an inscription written by a foreign hand upon a *tabula rasa*. The more ordinary compromise is that knowledge is partly *a priori* and partly *a posteriori*,—that we get facts from without, but "necessary ideas" from within. Now Hegel does not adopt either of the two opposing methods, nor yet the compromise between them. He maintains that all knowledge is *a posteriori* in one point of view, and that all knowledge is *a priori* in another. All is *a posteriori;* for no knowledge whatever is possible to the mind except through experience, and even its consciousness of self is possible only in relation to the not-self. Yet all knowledge is *a priori*, for this empirical process, which seems at first to be merely the introduction of foreign matter into the mind, is really its own evolution, and our highest knowledge is that in which we come to the consciousness of this ideal nature of things, and so transcend altogether the opposition of fact and idea.. Hegel is simply following the footsteps of Aristotle, who, though he continually insists that all knowledge is derived from experience, also declares that the mind is "potentially all that is knowable," and that "fully realised knowledge is identical with its object,"—*i.e.*, that the full development of the knowledge of the intelligible world, as such, is one with the evolution of thought to complete consciousness of self.

The reasons by which Hegel was led to this view will be evident if we go back for a moment to Kant. Kant appears to adopt the compromise that knowledge is partly *a priori* and partly *a posteriori;* but he secretly undermines it by the assertion that the *a priori* element is the *form*, and the *a posteriori* element the *matter*, of knowledge. For if by the form be meant the conditions under which the object is knowable, we cannot separate the *a posteriori* from the *a priori*. There are no "facts" as opposed to "ideas;" for the simplest fact we can mention already implies certain ideal principles, by which it is determined as a fact in relation to other facts and to the mind that knows it. The intelligence, in so far as it "makes nature," cannot be opposed to nature, as one object is opposed to another, for, so far, nature and intelligence are identical. Kant, however, confines the identity of nature and intelligence to certain general principles or laws, and supposes that beyond this there is a contingent element which is "given" to the intelligence under conditions of space and time, but not otherwise determined by it. Hence he thinks that the special laws which we discover in nature cannot be anticipated *a priori*, though the general principles of quantity, quality, and relation *can* be so anticipated. There is, therefore, so to speak, an *a posteriori* residuum in nature, or rather it is all *a posteriori* except the most general laws, to which the unity of knowing and being is limited. For though nature has in it all the content of mind, it has also a great deal more, which for mind is simply *a posteriori* matter of information, received from without, or at least from some unknown source.

Now Hegel carried out the unity of knowing and being, and so of *a priori* and *a posteriori*, to complete identity, by taking two steps beyond Kant, one of which has been indicated. In the first place, as we have seen, he added a new genus to Kant's genera of categories, the categories of "ideal unity;" or, what is the same thing from another side, he conceived the process of knowledge as including another stage beyond those enumerated by Kant—the stage, namely, of philosophy as distinguished from science, of reason as distinguished from reflection or understanding. In the second place, by the taking this step, Hegel was enabled to take another; for the categories of reason, and especially the idea of the unity of subject and object in which the 'Logic' ends, enabled Hegel to connect the forms of perception, space and time, with the forms of thought, in a way that was not possible for Kant, for whom the categories of reflection—categories like causality and reciprocity—were the last scientific determination of nature. In other words, Hegel's widened conception of the logical forms and processes enabled him to bridge over the gulf which, for Kant, separated the *a posteriori* from the *a priori*,—the manifold world of objects in time and space from the pure unity of thought or consciousness with itself. We can only indicate in a general way how this was possible.

So long as the laws of causality and reciprocity were conceived to be the ultimate principles of science, it was impossible that the gulf between the form and the matter of science should be filled up. These laws presuppose a matter which is external to themselves, and to the nature of which they afford us no clue. They are principles in accordance with which we investigate the relations of things, but which do not enable us to determine the *particular* nature of the things so related. The complete application of these principles, therefore, and the discovery of the laws of nature by means of them, seems still to leave the intelligence outside of the things it thus comes to know. The laws of gravitation, of chemical affinity, of electric polarity, seem still to be purely objective truths, indifferent and external to the mind that apprehends them. They may awake in the imagination an anticipation or presentment of the unity of nature and spirit, but they do not clearly reveal that unity to the understanding. But it is different when we begin to apply such categories as self-determination, final causality, organic unity, and the like. In that which is in any sense self-determined, the intelligence recognises its counterpart. Such a recognition, taking place in an immediate and unreflecting way, is what unites self-conscious beings to each other, and, in a minor sense, to all living beings. In man's earliest consciousness of the world, indeed, no distinct line is drawn between what has consciousness and what has merely life, or between what has life and what has not. The advance of reflection, however, gradually narrows the familiar world, as it intensifies man's consciousness of what he himself is, and his sense of difference from the rest of the universe. He becomes accustomed to regard objects as determined not by themselves, but by other objects, until to modern science this mode of viewing them seems the only natural one, and instead of finding its own freedom in the world, the mind rather begins to consider itself, like all other objects, as subjected to the law of external necessity. So conceiving of itself as well as of everything else, or rather regarding the universe as one in which, strictly speaking, there is no self present whatever, the intelligence is, as it were, estranged from itself and the world. Nature and human nature have both alike become for it mere objects without any subject, though the real objectivity and necessity of man's life is strangely perplexed by an illusion of freedom. Consciousness, as Professor Huxley represents it, is the occasional inactive spectator of a world with which it has nothing to do, and in which it falsely imagines itself to have the power to do anything. So far from finding *itself*, its own subjectivity, in the objective world which it observes, the intelligence finds nothing but an object even in itself.

Now the application of such categories as "self-determination" or "organic unity" to the world, still more the recognition that in these categories is found "the truth" or ultimate meaning of all other categories, involves a complete inversion of this way of thinking. It involves the denial of external necessity as the final explanation of anything, and teaches us to seek for self-determination, not only in self-conscious beings and animals, but, in a sense, even in what we call dead matter. It makes us regard the world as an organism in which even what is termed by distinction the inorganic is a vital part or organ. The partial prevalence of this mode of thought is shown by the tendency of this century, as contrasted with the last, to regard human society as an organism,—a whole in which there is some kind of unity or self which is present in every part,—and not as a mere collection of units externally related to each other. Very often this tendency is accompanied by an imperfect analysis of the idea of organism, which practically degrades it to the category of "reciprocal influence;" so that a writer who insists on the organic nature of society, will sometimes be found all but denying that an animal is anything more than the resultant of the action and reaction of its parts. A Comtist, however, who tells us that "the family," or that "humanity," is a reality, but who vehemently attacks the doctrine that "the soul" is anything but an abstraction, should look well to the security of the branch upon which he is sitting. The soul is an abstraction in the same sense as the family is an abstraction—*i.e.*,

Comtist view of Humanity. 193

it does not exist *without* the members, but as a living principle of self-determination *in* them; but the members also are "abstractions" without *it*. The imperfect realisation of what is involved in a category does not, however, affect the truth of the "instinct of reason," which leads to its application. It proves only that categories which rule the mind are, as not seldom happens, at war with those of which it is distinctly conscious.

The Comtist conception of humanity as an organism in an inorganic world — a world to which man as an organism is not essentially related, but which, in spite of, and even by reason of, its opposition, he gradually subordinates to his own needs, or turns into an instrument for the realisation of himself—is a temporary compromise of philosophy. And, like other compromises, it does complete justice to neither of the opposite modes of thought which it would combine,—neither to the *necessary relation* between man and the medium in which he lives, nor to the *self-determination* of men in relation to that medium. To do such justice is possible only when it is seen, in the sense explained in the last chapter, that "the truth of necessity is freedom." In other words, the ultimate explanation of things is to be found only when we take into account the fact that they are essentially related to the intelligence for which they exist, and when we recognise that all that so exists *for* intelligence is essentially a manifestation *of* intelligence. The object—and all things that exist are objects—is that in opposition, yet in relation, to which the subject is conscious of self. It is a form of the life of the subject, and it can be that, only as it has something of the ideal nature of the subject in itself. For a self-determined principle is, as we have seen, one that is determined, only as its *self* is present in all its determinations; or, to put the same idea in another form, an organic unity is one in which the whole is in every part. When, therefore, we once recognise that relation to the conscious subject or self is essential to every object, we are forced, at the same time, to conceive it—like the organ of a living body—as having a certain independent self-centred being in itself; for only so can it form an element in the life of intelligence. Thus the spiritual or ideal meaning of things is their ultimate meaning—that in which the secret of their existence is to be sought. They are real only as they are ideal. The scientific interpretation of things in which they are referred to themselves, and regarded as independent of thought, must therefore be subjected to a reinterpretation, in which we correct the abstraction involved in that way of looking at them, and regard them also in their relation to thought. But this new interpretation is so far from taking away their independence, or reducing them, according to the common view of idealism, to "mere ideas," or phenomena of a subjective consciousness, that rather it, for the first time, enables us to attribute to them a real independence—a being which is centred in itself. For while the ordinary scientific idea of the world as a system in which everything is determined from without according to the principles of causality, annihilates all distinctions and turns all the individuality of things into a semblance, the idea of the world as an organic system whose centre lies in a self-conscious intelligence breaks up this levelling fatalism, and reveals in every existence a centre of self-individualising energy. Where, therefore, science seemed to turn all things—even life and intelligence itself—into dead matter, which moves only as it is moved by another, philosophy, guided by this new idea, is enabled to find life even in that which is inorganic and dead. While to the former the facts and laws of the world are an absolute *a posteriori*, in which the intelligence cannot find itself, but which it must simply take as they are given, without hoping to understand their reason; to the latter there are no facts which are not at heart ideas,—no reality of nature or spirit which can permanently remain as an irreducible surd, an external and incomprehensible datum, for the intelligence. The *a posteriori* is but the *a priori* in the making. In this sense there is no presumption in the strong words of Hegel: "The nature of the universe, hidden and shut up in itself as it is at first, has no power which can permanently resist the courageous efforts of the intelligence: it must at last open itself up; it must reveal all its depth and riches to the spirit, and surrender them to be enjoyed by it." For this is but saying that the world is essentially intelligible, and therefore may ultimately be seen in its unity with the intelligence.

At the same time this must not be interpreted as if it involved anything of what is commonly meant by an *a priori* construction of the world. Hegel is well aware that there is a "hard husk" to break through ere it is possible to reach the ideal meaning of things, and he is aware also that this "hard husk" must be broken by science, ere it can be finally dissolved by philosophy. In other words, he is aware that the external contingency in which things present themselves to the ordinary consciousness, as simply existing side by side in space, and happening contemporaneously or successively in time, must yield to the scientific determination of them in their laws and causes, ere it is possible for philosophy to discover in them the organic manifestation of intelligence. "The philosophy of nature takes up the matter, which physical science has prepared out of experience, at the point where science leaves it, without looking back to experience for its verification. Science, therefore, must work into the hands of philosophy, that philosophy in turn may translate the universality of reflection which science has produced into the higher universality of the reason, showing how the intelligible object evolves itself out of the intelligence as an organic whole, whose necessity is in itself. The philosophical way of presenting things is not a capricious effort, for once in a way, to walk upon one's head, as a change from the ordinary method of walking on one's feet—or to escape the monotony of one's ordinary face by painting it; but it is because the manner of science does not finally satisfy the intelligence that we are obliged to go beyond it."[1]

The "hard husk," however,—the contingency of space and time,—has itself its necessity in the nature of the intelligence to which it presents so much resistance, and which it seems often to baffle. This is a point on which there has often been a misunderstanding of the Hegelian system, but which is closely connected with its central idea. Thus Schelling objects to the dialectic by which Hegel passes from the Logic to the philosophy of nature, as a mere tissue of metaphors which conceal an absolute

[1] Hegel, vii. 18.

break in thought. And at first it is not easy to see more than this in Hegel's assertion that "the Idea freely lets itself go out of itself, while yet resting in itself, and remaining absolutely secure of itself;" or again, that "Nature is the extreme self-alienation (Entaüsserung) of spirit, in which it yet remains one with itself." If, however, the reader will recall what has already been said of the unity of opposites, and of a self-determined principle as being one that necessarily goes out of itself, or gives the utmost possible freedom to its determination, the obscurity and apparently metaphorical character of such expressions will partly disappear.

Nature is for Hegel that extreme of possible opposition to spirit through which, and through which alone, it can fully realise itself. We may make this clearer by a short reference to the treatment of this contrast in other philosophies. To the Cartesian school, nature and spirit, matter and mind, were absolute opposites, between which no link of connection could be detected, and which therefore were conceived to be connected only by the will of God. Mind was that which is undivided and indivisible—purely self-determined and active. Matter was that which is infinitely divisible and purely passive, or determined by another than itself. Each must therefore be explained entirely for itself, and without aid of the other. Yet they are bound together by the inexplicable and incomprehensible relation of each to God, who, though spiritual, yet acts upon the essentially passive matter, and imparts to it activity and motion, and who determines the essentially self-determined mind to apprehend the phases of this alien matter.

A similar opposition strangely reappears in the philosophy of Mr Herbert Spencer, who holds that the world is presented to us in two ways—as a series of motions of matter and as a series of feelings or ideas of mind; but that we are unable to bring these two views together, or to penetrate to the unknown reality which is beneath both. Now there can be no doubt that, as Descartes saw, mind and matter are opposites; but as they are correlative opposites and so necessarily united, it is not necessary to seek for any *Deus ex machina* to bring them together. Mind or self-consciousness "overreaches," as Hegel says, this opposition of itself to that which is opposed to it as its object; or, to put it from the other side, a self-conscious principle can reveal itself as a self-determined principle only in this extreme opposition, and in overcoming it. The "free" existence of the world as an external aggregate of objects in space, with no appearance of relation to mind, and the "free" existence of each object in the world, as external to the other objects and merely in contingent relation to them, are characteristics which belong to these objects just because they are the manifestations of a self-determined principle, which can realise itself only as it goes out of itself, or gives itself away, but which in this "self-alienation" remains "secure of itself and resting in itself." On the other hand, this security of intelligence in the freedom of its object is possible just because its own nature is what it has given to the object, which therefore, in realising itself, must return to its source. The movement or process of the external world, thus freed or left to itself in its externality, can only be to go *into* itself, or to "sublate" or remove its own externality, and so to return to that unity which seems to have abandoned it, and which it seems at first to have abandoned. It is not merely, therefore, that the contingency of nature is discovered by science to be the mask or disguise of necessity, and this necessity again by philosophy is detected to be the mask or disguise of freedom. This of itself would be merely a subjective process of knowledge, without any objective movement corresponding to it in nature, and thus the self-alienation or self-manifestation of the mind in nature would be reduced to an illusion. But nature itself, regarded as independent of intelligence, is this process "writ large," and fixed in the form of an external hierarchy of existences, which in their relation and subordination exhibit the successive stages of development by which the object returns to the subject. In its mechanical, chemical, and vital substances, nature presents to us, though still in the form of externality, the various steps of the process whereby this independence of things of each other and of the intelligence, as it were, refutes and transcends itself. In the inorganic world the ideal principle is present as an inner or hidden nature of things, a law of relation between parts external to each other, which manifests itself only as these external parts, in their notions and changes, continually betray the secret of their essential relativity to each other. In the living being, however, this inner nature does not merely *underlie* the fixed difference of external parts, but is *revealed* in them as a principle of organisation, continually distributing itself to them as members of one body, which can maintain their independence only as they make themselves subordinate to the common life. Thus in life we have the differentiating and integrating movement of thought expressed in outward form; and

Hegel therefore calls it the *ideality* of nature—that in which the external, as it were, visibly contradicts and refutes its own externality. But this idealisation is still imperfect, for it is not conscious of itself; it is not present to the living being itself, but only to us. Nature rises to self-consciousness only in man, who thus becomes conscious not only of it, but of himself in distinction from and in relation to it; and who, in the process of his development, has to overcome this still remaining antagonism between himself and the world, or between consciousness and self-consciousness, and so to realise his unity and the unity of all things and beings with the absolute spirit "in whom they live, and move, and have their being."

Such is the general outline which Hegel seeks to fill up by his philosophy of nature and spirit. In the former part of his task, in dealing with nature, and especially with the inorganic world, he is least successful. Obviously, if we adopt Hegel's view, it will be more difficult to trace the ideal meaning of nature, which is the idea in its extreme self-alienation, than of spirit, in which it is returning to itself. The general necessity of such an external realisation of the ideal principle under conditions of space and time it is not difficult to comprehend, and it is easy also to detect a link of analogy which runs through all nature, and makes it into a continual illustration of ideal relations. "Nature," as Novalis said, "is a kind of illuminated table of the contents of the spirit." Gravitation, chemical affinity, vital nutrition, may be all used as pictures of the processes of intellectual and moral life, and many so-called philosophical theories have been little more than logical developments of the consequences of such metaphors. Poetry, again, is often little more than a continual playing upon the latent accords that bind all forms of existence together. When, however, it is attempted to turn such poetry into philosophy, to discover what exactly is the identity that lies beneath these analogies, and to follow logically the filiation and connection of its changes of form, the "hard husk" is found difficult to penetrate, and it must be the more difficult the lower the existence we are examining in the scale of being—*i.e.*, the further it is from the nature of spirit. Hence it is the simplest things of nature with which it is hardest for an ideal philosophy to deal. The physical is harder for it than the chemical, the chemical than the vital, for the same reason which makes poetry prefer life to death. The idealistic interpretation of nature is therefore exposed to serious difficulties and dangers, especially in the region of mechanics and physics; and indeed it cannot be successfully attempted at all till science has carried *its* interpretation to an advanced stage. Attempted earlier, it is apt to become little better than a systematic and therefore lifeless kind of poetry, which intuitively grasps at a unity it cannot yet define. Of this character, probably, is much of Hegel's philosophy of nature. Science in these departments had not reached the point which, as Hegel himself maintained, it must reach, before the categories of reason could be applied to them; and his own knowledge of physics and chemistry was at best second-hand. He devoted, indeed, comparatively little of his attention to such subjects: all that he published on the Philosophy of Nature was the outline in the Encyclopædia, which, with the addition of some notes taken from his Lectures, makes one volume of his works. The principles of the 'Logic' were used by him for the most part as a key to the life of man, and especially to his highest spiritual experiences, in morality, art, and religion. Thus it is upon "the first and the last things"—upon the metaphysical principles in which philosophy begins, and upon that highest idealisation of man's life in which it ends—that the main lights of the Hegelian philosophy are cast. The intermediate regions of nature, and of human life so far as it is most closely linked with nature, are only briefly sketched, and remain on the whole a desideratum. In spite of his encyclopædic industry, Hegel had not the impartial exhaustive curiosity of Aristotle, and preferred to direct his thought to those objects in which the ideal meaning is most easily read. His speculation therefore, like Plato's, was predominantly guided — at least where it goes beyond the sphere of abstract metaphysic — by the practical instincts of the higher life of man, by the desire to restore the moral and religious basis of human existence, which a revolutionary scepticism had destroyed. To this the Lectures, which form the greater part of his works, are devoted. It must, however, be remembered that we have these Lectures in a form which was never authorised by Hegel himself, and that they were compiled after his death, mainly from the notes of students who were among his audience. Even if we could always depend upon the verbal accuracy of the report, it is obvious that such discourses, delivered with reference to the needs of the hearers, rather than to a complete discussion of the subject, cannot be regarded in the same light as works like the 'Logic,' which came from his hand as a completely reasoned system. Their informality and discursive character, however, if it takes from their authority as expressions of the author's mind and from their value as scientific treatises, has some compensating advantages, if we regard them as a means of education in philosophy; for in this point of view their very artlessness gives them something of the same stimulating suggestive power which is attained by the consummate art of the Platonic Dialogues.

To follow out in detail any of these applications of the principle of Hegel would be beyond the scope of the present volume. It may, however, be desirable to indicate, more fully than has yet been done, how it was that Hegel could regard this principle as in a special sense Christian, and even as identical with the essential idea of Christianity.

In an earlier chapter it has been shown how Hegel at first found in Greek literature and Greek life that unity of the ideal with the real, of the freedom of spirit with the necessity of nature, which Kant and Fichte seemed to deny. In the State the Greek saw, not a mere external authority, but only the realisation of his own freedom; and in the gods he worshipped, not a foreign and despotic power, but only the ideal unity of the natural and social organism in which he was a member. He was at home in the little world in which he lived and moved, which his spirit had made, and was continually remaking. For him, the division of "self" and "not-self" had "passed in music out of sight,"—had been overcome unconsciously without even being thought of; for the spirit of his city was, as it were, the "substance," the presupposed substratum, of his consciousness of himself. Yet just herein, as Hegel came to see, lay the fragility, the imperfection, the transitory character, of the Greek reconciliation of man with the world. It was not based on any deep consciousness of the antagonism of the inner and outer life, or of a spiritual process by which that antagonism could be overcome. It was a gift received from the hands of nature,—which was in itself a contradiction, for the spirit cannot accept gifts except from itself, and a possession ceases to be spiritual by the very fact that it is not spiritually achieved. As soon, therefore, as reflection suggested the idea of a division between the individual and his world, at that moment the unity disappeared; for it was not based on reason,—on any consciousness of a unity which transcended the division,—but rather on an unconsciousness of the division itself. Hence even the idealisation of this unconscious reconciliation in Art and Poetry, by making it into an object and dealing with it freely as such, tended to disturb it, and to substitute for it that consciousness of the self in its loneliness and opposition to the world, which is expressed in the individualistic philosophy of the Stoics, Epicureans, and Sceptics. The Aristophanic comedy may be regarded as the last happy moment of the Greek spirit, its last triumphant consciousness of self, in which it rejoices over a "world turned upside down," over the perversion of all the ideal and real forms of its existence. But this happy moment rapidly passes into the stern, self-centred life of the Stoic, who withdraws from the world into the fortress of his own soul,—into the hard prose of Roman life, in which the only social bond is the legal relation of persons,—and finally into the despair of the sceptic, who, doubting everything, is driven in the end to doubt himself, and regarding everything objective as an empty appearance, is forced at last to recognise the very consciousness of self as an illusion. For the division of man from the world is his division from himself, and when he shuts himself up within his own soul, he finds there nothing but emptiness and vanity. What, then, was to heal this division, to reconcile man to the world and to himself, and to bring back that joyful consciousness which Greece had lost? The problem is one for the present day, as well as for the earlier days of the Roman empire; for now even more than then, the intense sense of personality, of subjective freedom, has disturbed man's consciousness of unity with the world, and thrown him back upon himself, only to awake in him a painful sense of emptiness and weakness, and a longing for what seems an impossible deliverance from himself.

In the following passage of his earlier work, 'The 'Phænomenology,' Hegel paints the disease, and hints at its cure, in words in which poetry and speculation are wonderfully united :—

"The Stoic independence of thought, passing through the movement of scepticism, finds its true meaning revealed in a consciousness—which is at the same time a despair—of self. To this despairing self-consciousness is revealed the hollowness both of the real claims vindicated for the abstract person in Roman law, and also of the ideal claims vindicated for the thinking self in Stoicism. It has learnt that the claims so vindicated are in truth entirely lost; that the self so asserted is rather absolutely estranged from itself. Its despair, therefore, may be regarded as the counterpart and completion of that triumphant joy with which the spirit of Comedy in Aristophanes rejoices in itself, looking down upon the annihilation of all that which is *not the self*. For while in this comic consciousness all objective reality is alienated from itself and emptied of substantial worth in relation to the self; the despair that follows upon scepticism is the tragic fate which immediately falls upon the self which thus in its isolation has raised itself to the absolute. It is the consciousness of the loss of all reality in the assurance of the self, and again of the loss of this last assurance,—it is that agony of desertion which expresses itself in the hard saying that *God is dead*.

"Thus, then, the ethical life of the ancient State has disappeared in the legality of Rome, as the religion which idealised that State has vanished in Comedy, and the despairing self-consciousness is simply the knowledge of all that has been lost. For it,—as we have seen,—neither the immediate dignity and value of the individual, nor that secondary ideal value which he received from thought, any longer exists. Trust in the eternal laws of the gods is silenced, like the oracles by which they revealed particular events to men. The statues worshipped in earlier religion are now dead stones, whose inspiring soul has departed, and the hymns of praise that were sung to them are become words in which no one believes. The tables of the gods are without spiritual meat and drink, and from the games and festivals no longer does the spirit of man receive back the joyful sense of his unity with the divine. The works of the Muse are now deserted by that spiritual force which drew the assurance of itself even out of the very annihilation of all glory of gods and men. These works have already become— what they are for us now—fair fruits broken away from the tree, which a friendly fate has conveyed to us, as a maiden might present those fruits; for with the fruits she cannot give us the real life on which their existence depended, not the tree that bore them, not the earth and the elements from which they drew their substance, not the climate which gave them their peculiar character, nor the vicissitude of the seasons that ruled over the process of their growth. In like manner, the fate which has preserved for us the works of antique art does not bring with them the world to which they belonged—not the spring and summer of that ethical life in which they blossomed and ripened, but only a dim remembrance of such a reality. Our enjoyment of them is not, therefore, an act of divine worship in which our consciousness reaches its complete and satisfying truth; it is only the external service which washes away from their purity any drops of rain or particles of dust that may adhere to them, and which, in place of the inner constituents of the ethical life which produced and inspired them, raises up an endless scaffolding of the dead elements of their outward existence,—the language, the historical circumstances, &c., which throw light upon them. Our end also in all this service is, not to give our own life to them, but merely to set them up as pictures before our imagination. But yet, as the maiden who presents the plucked fruits is more than the nature which first produced them, with all its conditions and elements—the tree, the air, the light, &c.—since in a higher way she gathers all this together in the light of the self-conscious eye, and the expression of the offering gesture; so the spirit of the fate which presents us with these works of art is more than all that was attained in that ancient national existence, for it is the realisation in us as an inward life of the spirit which in them was still outward and external; it is the spirit of the tragic fate, which gathers all those individualised gods and attributes of the divine substance into one Pantheon, the spirit which is conscious in itself of its own spiritual nature."[1]

"The spirit that is conscious of itself as spirit." This to Hegel is the solution of the difficulty in which the individualism of ancient and of modern times has involved itself. Its value will be understood only if we have the difficulty itself clearly before us. The dualism

[1] Hegel, ii. 544-546.

between the object and subject—between man and his world—which the Stoic sought to escape by withdrawing into himself, follows him, as the sceptic showed, even into the inner life. The soul opposed to the world and emptied of it, is found to be opposed to and emptied of itself. It finds no inner wealth to console it in its barren self-assertion. As the Roman citizen, invested by law with absolute rights of person and property, found no security for them except in the mere will and brute force of the emperor, and thus in practice his absolute freedom converted itself into absolute slavery; so in like manner the Stoic consciousness of the absolute worth and dignity of the rational life which is present to each individual, needed but a little maturing — a deeper realisation of its own meaning — to pass into an abject self-despair, into a sense of infinite want, and into a superstitious readiness to accept any outward oracle or revelation which might deliver it from its own inward emptiness. So again, in modern times, those nations who have come to regard every kind of law and fixed institution as a foreign yoke, and to seek for freedom in nihilism and universal revolt, have often been found ready, in the inevitable weariness of their own caprice, to accept any despotism that will free them from themselves. And those men who have most deeply been imbued by the modern spirit of subjectivity, which knows no authority but itself and opposes its own inner light to all external teachings of experience, have not unfrequently been driven in the end to save themselves from the waywardness and vacuity of mysticism by subjecting themselves to the outward rule of an authoritative Church. Such changes are not accidents; they are simply the natural development of the consciousness of self. They show, in the "logic of facts," that extreme subjectivity and individualism contains in itself its own contradiction, as the acorn contains the oak. Give it only the necessary conditions and opportunities of growth, and this is what it must result in.

The lesson to be learnt from this rapid conversion of the merely subjective into the merely objective, is not that the truth lies in the latter apart from the former. The cure for diseases of rationalism and scepticism is not implicit faith, any more than despotism is the cure for revolution. The assertion of reason and liberty,—of the subject as against the object in which he was hitherto lost,—was a great step in the spiritual development of man; and any effort to recover the intellectual and moral harmony of the inward and the outward life, which should begin by withdrawing from the position thus gained, would be essentially reactionary, and, in the end, futile. For reaction cannot again restore the unity as it existed before the distinction and opposition were seen; all that it can do is to put the object, as opposed to the subject, in place of the subject as opposed to the object—in other words, to pass from one extreme to another, which is equally imperfect and self-contradictory. Implicit faith, by its sacrifice of reason, cannot restore the first unity of the mind with its object, which the assertion of "private judgment" has broken; rather it will be a unity of slavery, whereas that first unity was imperfect freedom. Or, to take another example, empiricism cannot furnish a correction for that subjective idealism which arises out of the first imperfect interpretation of the truth, that all objects are essentially related to the subject that knows them. It will only be equivalent to a resolve to forget the inconvenient fact of the subjectivity of knowledge, and to treat things *as if* they were entirely independent of mind. In these and all similar cases, when the distinction or opposition is once made, the only real escape from its power, and so from the assertion of one of the opposed elements at the expense of the other, is to find the *limit* of the opposition, or the point where it gives way to unity. And that there is a point where it will so give way, is already manifest from the fact, that each of the opposites, if taken as absolute, involves its own contradiction.

What was fatal to the Greek state, and with it to all the political and religious life of the ancient world, was the assertion that man, as a rational or self-conscious being, is a law and an end to himself. In this it is involved that, ultimately, he can know and obey nothing but himself. Taken in a one-sided and exclusive sense, this doctrine is the denial of all relation of the individual either in thought or action to anything but himself; but taken in this sense it contains, as we have seen, its own refutation, and passes into its opposite. The truth, however, is to be found by considering what this self-contradiction really means. It means, in the first place, that the opposition is a relative one, and that the self which is opposed to the world, even in such opposition, is essentially related to it. And it means, in the second place, that while the direct and immediate attempt to assert and realise the self as *against* the not-self is suicidal, there is a higher assertion and realisation of the self *in* and *through* the not-self, which, however, is possible only in so far as that first suicidal attempt is abandoned. The way to self-realisation is through self-renunciation—*i.e.*, through renunciation of that natural and immediate life of the self in which it is opposed to the not-self. Spiritual life is not like natural life—a direct development and outgoing of energy, which only at its utmost point of expansion meets with death as an external enemy, and in it finds its limit and its end. On the contrary, the life of a spiritual being, as such, is, in a true sense, a continual dying. Every step in it is won by a break with the immediate or natural self—the self which is opposed to the not-self; for only as this self dies can the higher self, which is in unity with the not-self, be developed. And, on the other hand, just for this reason there is for the spiritual self no absolute death. Because it is capable of dying to itself,—because, indeed, as will be more fully shown in the sequel, it cannot live but by some kind of dying to self,—it cannot in any final sense die. As it can make that which most seems to limit it a part of its own life, it has no absolute limit; it takes up death into itself as an element, and does not therefore need to fear it as an enemy.

Words like these will, no doubt, seem at first to be mystical and metaphorical to those who look at them in an external way. And, indeed, they fairly represent the usual language of Christian mysticism, or rather, we might say more truly, the universal language of the religious life of Christianity wherever that life has reached any real depth of self-consciousness—the language of St Paul and of St Augustine, of Thomas à Kempis and Martin Luther, as of men like Maurice and Campbell in our own day. Such language, however, though not denied to have a certain truth in its own sphere, is usually kept to that sphere, and not brought down into the region of the ordinary understanding, or weighed against the words and categories which hold good there. What is peculiar to Hegel is, that he brings the two regions together and compares them; that he weighs the vivid poetic utterance of spiritual intuition, and the prose of common life and of science, together in the same scales; and that he seeks to prove that, as exact and scientific definitions of the reality of things, the former has a higher truth than the latter. To him, therefore, the great aphorism, in which the Christian ethics and theology may be said to be summed up, that "he that saveth his life shall lose it, and he that loseth his life shall save it," is no mere epigrammatic saying, whose self-contradiction is not to be regarded too closely; it is rather the first distinct, though as yet undeveloped, expression of the exact truth as to the nature of spirit. To show how this is possible, it will be best, in the first place, to take the words in their immediate ethical meaning.

Taken, then, in its application to morals, the maxim, "Die to live," seems to combine the principle of asceticism with the principle of hedonism or utilitarianism; for while it points, like the latter, to a positive realisation of self, it implies, like the former, that the way to such self-realisation is through self-abnegation. Interpreted in a coarse external way, it might be supposed to mean only that this world must be sacrificed in order that the next may be won. But such an interpretation is equally imperfect on the side of the sacrifice and of the realisation. It is imperfect on the side of the sacrifice; for a mere giving up of a present for a future satisfaction is far from being a real giving up of the self; it is only a substitution of "other-worldliness" for "worldliness," and selfishness is not overcome by its gratification being postponed. And it is imperfect on the side of the realisation; for it is not the life of this world, the life renounced, which is regained, but a life in another world which is supposed to be utterly different from it. The true interpretation of the maxim is, that the individual must die to an isolated life,—*i.e.*, a life for and in himself, a life in which the immediate satisfaction of desire as his desire is an end in itself,—in order that he may live the spiritual life, the universal life which really belongs to him as a spiritual or self-conscious being. Now it is a simple psychological fact that, as we cannot know ourselves except in relation to objects from which we distinguish ourselves, so we cannot seek our own pleasure except in objects which are distinguishable from that pleasure, and which we desire for themselves. Desire always in the first instance looks outward to the object, and only indirectly through the object at the self; pleasure comes of the realisation of desire, but the desire is primarily for something else than the pleasure; and though it may gradually become tinctured by the consciousness of the subjective result, it can never entirely lose its objective reference. The pleasure-seeker is an abstraction: for just in proportion as we approximate to the state of the pure hunter for pleasures, for whom all objective interest is lost in mere self-seeking, it is demonstrable by the nature of the case, and shown by experience, that for us all pleasure must cease. As it is a condition of our intellectual life that we exist for ourselves only as other things and beings exist for us, so it is a condition of our practical life that we can realise ourselves or live for ourselves only as we live for other ends and beings than ourselves. Thus it appears that there is an element of self-negation even in our most immediate theoretical and practical existence, and that we must die to live—go out of ourselves to be ourselves—even in the most sensuous and selfish life we can possibly live. Obviously, however, this does not take away the significance of the principle as a moral law, but rather for the first time shows the possibility of obeying it, as a law which is grounded in the real nature of man: a law under which we not only *ought* to live, but under which we *must* in some measure live, if as rational beings we are to live at all. We are thus also enabled to remove a misconception which in many minds stands in the way of the acceptance of the principle of self-sacrifice, as if it involved a mere ascetic self-annihilation or a rejection of all the positive elements in life. In view of such a negative interpretation of the principle, we can easily understand how many should be prepared, with Bentham, to denounce the ascetic as a superstitious believer in the "universal misery theory," and to declare with Spinoza that philosophy "should be the meditation not of death, but of life." But when it is seen that all that is really positive in our life has, in the sense of the principle, a negative element in it, and that it is only through such negation of self that any positive good can ever be attained, it can no longer be apprehended that the *further* development of this negative or self-renouncing aspect of morality will impoverish human life, or strip it of any of its real sources of joy. In truth, the abstract distinction drawn between positive self-gratification and negative self-denial—which is at the basis of the ordinary opposition of asceticism and hedonism — is essentially mistaken; for, in the sense of the distinction, there are no pure pleasures possible to man. What we have is always a positive mediated by a negative; and if we could absolutely sever either from the other, we should come in both cases to the same result. The absolute pleasure-seeker would, by the opposite road, reach the same goal with the absolute ascetic — the extinction of all desire and pleasure. On the other hand, the same line of thought enables us to see that the wider and completer is the good—*i.e.*, the realisation of ourselves—which we seek, the deeper and more thorough must be the negation of self on which it is based. "More life and fuller, *that* we want;" but by a law that cannot be defeated or cheated, this fuller life is possible to us only through the sacrifice, renunciation, or death of the immediate or natural self—the self which is opposed to the not-self—and which seeks a good for itself which is not a good for others. For it is only in breaking down the boundary that separates our life from the life of others, that we can at the same time break down the boundary which prevents their life from becoming ours. St Paul's saying, "All things are yours, for ye are God's," expresses the true conditions on which alone the limits of the individual life can be removed—viz., that it should cease to will itself except through the whole of which it is a part.

The principle that he who loses his life in this sense saves it, has, however, another application. It is already seen to be true, in so far as life is measured by its interests, and in so far as even the pains and sorrows of the wider life contain a kind of compensation in them, which makes them rather to be chosen than the narrower joys. " We can only have the highest happiness —such as goes along with being a great man—by having wide thoughts, and much feeling for the rest of the world as well as ourselves; and this sort of happiness often brings so much pain with it that we can only tell it from pain by its being what we would choose before everything else, because our souls see it is good."[1] But this inward compensation might seem to be reconcilable with a constitution of the universe in which all that we call higher interests were, after all, sacrificed to an adverse or indifferent fate. Really, however, it is not so reconcilable; for "morality," as it has been said, " is the nature of things." The innate law of spiritual life cannot fail of its effect outwardly, any more than inwardly. To suppose that it could so fail would be to suppose that a spiritual being is simply one finite existence beside the others, which must "take its chance" with them in the struggle for existence. This, however, is just that view of things of which the whole process of thought, expressed in the Hegelian philosophy, is the refutation. For what Hegel sought to show is, that the intelligible world is not only, as Kant declared, essentially related to the intelligence for which it exists, but that, as a consequence of this, it is in itself nothing but the manifestation of intelligence. In a world which is essentially spiritual, it is impossible to conceive that the existence of spiritual beings should be a means to an external end, or a link like the other links in the chain of causation. And it is equally

[1] George Eliot—Romola, iii. 290.

impossible that in such a world the essential law of spiritual life should not be the truth that underlies, overreaches, and interprets all other laws. The moral principle that we must lose our lives in order to save them, has therefore its counterpart and complement in a law of the universe, according to which all the evils and sorrows that belong to the development of the spiritual life—(and in a world which is in its essence spiritual, this ultimately means all evils and sorrows whatever)—contain in them "the promise and the potency" of a good, in which they are not merely compensated, but taken up and transcended. "The wounds of the spirit can be healed, so that not even a scar remains." "Die to live," is a principle which can be true only for a being for whom, as has been said, there is no absolute death, but in all death the means of a higher life. Now it is just this belief which constitutes the Christian optimism, that "all things work together for good." Pessimism is based on the idea that evil is a necessary and absolute existence; and a modified optimism, which opposes it merely by dwelling on the positive side of life—on the fact, or supposed fact, *e.g.*, that there are numbers of people who are tolerably happy, and that in most lives there is a balance of pleasure over pain—is very far from being a satisfactory answer to it. The only satisfactory answer must lie in the perception of the essentially relative character of evil and sorrow itself, and this is what is implied in the words "shall save it." The Christian optimism is the recognition that in a spiritual world a spiritual being, as such, cannot find an absolute limit or foreign necessity, against which his life must be broken in pieces; but that, on the contrary, all apparent outward limits, and even death itself, are for it but the means to a higher freedom and realisation of self. The Christian theology is, in its essence, little more than the development of this idea; for its primary doctrine is that God—the absolute principle to which, as their unity, we must refer all things and beings—is a "Spirit,"—*i.e.*, a Being whose life is self-determination and self-revelation — a self-revelation which includes also the element of self-sacrifice. For, as we have seen, the communication or giving out of life, which is involved in the idea of such a Being, cannot stop short of the communication of *a self*, and so of *Himself* to His creatures, which are thus "made partakers of the divine nature." Or, to put it otherwise, what Christianity teaches is only that the law of the life of spirit—the law of self-realisation through self-abnegation — holds good for God as for man, and, indeed, that the spirit that works in man to "die to live" is the Spirit of God. For Hegel such a doctrine was the demonstrated result of the whole idealistic movement which is summed up in his Logic. So far, then, as Christianity means this, it was not in any spirit of external accommodation that he tried to connect his doctrine with it. Rather it was the discovery of this as the essential meaning of Christianity, which first enabled him to recognise it as the ultimate lesson of the idealistic movement of thought in Kant, Fichte, and Schelling.

The Hegelian philosophy, some of the main aspects of which we have attempted to exhibit, is so comprehensive in its range of thought, and it is the product of a time still so near our own, that it is not yet easy, or perhaps even possible, to fix its permanent value as an element in philosophical culture. The tendencies and ideas, which it attempts to bring to a unity, are still striving for the mastery around us and within us; and the sifting process, by which a principle is gradually delivered from the accidents of its first expression, and from the misunderstandings and prejudices which are due to such accidents, is yet far from being completed. When Hegel died, his philosophy held all but undisputed predominance in Berlin and the other Prussian universities; and, in spite of the protest which Schelling and others kept up against it, it was generally acknowledged as the greatest intellectual influence in all the scientific schools of Germany. The criticisms to which it had as yet been subjected were so superficial, or based on such obvious misunderstanding, that the faith of Hegel's disciples was as yet put to no very hard test: nor could it be said that there was much arrogance in his own attitude when, after repelling one or two feeble attacks upon his principles, he used the language of the great Frederic in reference to the half-barbarous Pandours by whom he was so often beset: "This is the sort of fry with which I have to keep struggling." But after the death of Hegel all this was gradually changed. By the publication of his Lectures, the doctrine was at last set before the world in its completed form—in all its manifold applications. Criticism soon began to penetrate beyond the outworks, and to assail the central ideas of the system; and the master was no longer there to repel the attack with crushing dialectic, and to turn it into a means of throwing new light upon his principles. In the Hegelian school itself, the affinities of different minds for different aspects of so comprehensive a system began to disturb the unity and balance of elements which Hegel had established. There were some for whom the main value of the philosophy lay in its results—in the return to religious faith and social morality which it seemed to make possible: and such minds were sometimes apt to forget that reconstruction is not merely restoration, and that it was only by developing the principle of freedom itself that Hegel was able to discover the sound and permanent elements in the institutions and traditions of the past. Those who thus mistook or narrowed the principle of development into a defence of things established, were gradually gathered into a more or less homogeneous group under the name of the "Hegelian Right." On the other hand, there were those to whom the idea of freedom, and the negative dialectic by which it was developed, seemed the one important element in Hegel; and for them Hegelianism tended to become only a more effective and profound expression of the spirit which had already manifested its power in the *Aufklärung* and the Revolution. This group formed what was known as the "Hegelian Left." Thus, just as the death of Socrates was the signal for the rise of a number of antagonistic sects, each of which grasped only a fragment of the master's doctrine, but gave it a fuller development than the master had done, and set it in direct opposition to the other fragments,—so within the Hegelian school a division of tendency now showed itself, so wide and far-reaching, that the same principles which, on the one side, were interpreted as the defence of orthodoxy and reactionary politics, were used on the other side for the support of atheism and nihilism. And as usually happens in the divisions of religion and politics, there was soon an increasing number of observers who drew from the controversy a proof that Hegelianism, or even philosophy itself, contained in it no living scientific principle of unity, but was merely a confused syncretism of opinions, which might be held together for a moment by a *tour de force* of genius, but which necessarily fell asunder as soon as the master's hand was removed. Such a scepticism is a natural and frequently recurring phenomenon of man's spiritual life, by reason of the antagonisms through which it develops, and it can be overcome only by a deeper consciousness of the nature and laws of that development. There is, however, no reason for wonder or despair as to the essential truth of the principles of the Hegelian philosophy in the fact that it has gone, or is going, through the same phases of life which have been traversed by the ideas of Socrates, by the Christian religion, and indeed by every living principle which has profoundly influenced the mind of man. Hegel himself has interpreted his own fate for us. " A party first truly shows itself to have won the victory when it breaks up into two parties: for so it proves that it contains in itself the principle with which at first it had to conflict, and thus that it has got beyond the one-sidedness which was incidental to its earliest expression. The interest which formerly divided itself between it and that to which it was opposed now falls entirely within itself, and the opposing principle is left behind and forgotten, just because it is represented by one of the sides in the new controversy which now occupies the minds of men. At the same time, it is to be observed that when the old principle thus reappears, it is no longer what it was before; for it is changed and purified by the higher element into which it is now taken up. In this point of view, that discord which appears at first to be a lamentable breach and dissolution of the unity of a party, is really the crowning proof of its success."[1] In other words, such discord is the proof of vitality; for it is the conflict of elements which, in spite of their apparently absolute antagonism, are really held within the unity of one life, and which, therefore, must be reconciled by its further development.

That the form and the matter of Hegel—the dialectical process and the positive or constructive result of his philosophy—can thus be set against each other, proves nothing more than what a survey of his work has already shown us, — viz., that the development of that philosophy in Hegel's own works is very incomplete; or, to put it in a slightly different point of view, that the application of the principle expressed in the Hegelian Logic to the complex facts of nature and history, was only imperfectly carried out by him. Hence the sifting affinity, —by which the new principle, like a germinating seed, draws to itself the fruitful elements of the life of the past, while it repels all that is merely traditional and dead,—is apt to show itself in an alternation or opposition of negative and positive, sceptical and constructive tendencies in different minds; which may thus often appear as irreconcilable enemies, though they are really the organs of one spiritual life, and the ministers of its development.

It is sometimes said that in Germany Hegel's philosophy has entirely lost the credit which it partially retains

[1] Hegel, ii. 420.

in other countries. And indeed, if by adherence to Hegel be meant that kind of discipleship which is content to be labelled with the name of Hegelian as a complete indication of all its ideas and tendencies, we might state the fact still more generally. For there are few, if any, in any country, who could now take up the same position towards Hegel which was accepted by his immediate disciples. To us, at this distance of time, Hegel, at the highest, can be only the last great philosopher who deserves to be placed on the same level with Plato and Aristotle in ancient, and with Spinoza and Kant in modern times, and who, like them, has given an "epoch-making" contribution to the development of the philosophic, or, taking the word in the highest sense, the idealistic, interpretation of the world. In other words, he can only be the last writer who has made a vitally important addition to the proof, that those ideas, which are at the root of poetry and religion, are also principles of science. But, like these earlier philosophies, like every other spiritual influence, the Hegelian philosophy has to die that it may live; to break away from the accidents of its first immediate form, that it may become an element in the growing life of man. And this means that, to a certain extent, it is ceasing to be possible to regard it as a separate product, the value or truth of which can be weighed by itself. For any one whose view is not limited by words or superficial appearances, it is not difficult to see that, in the scientific life of Germany as of other countries, there is no greater power at present than Hegelianism, especially in all that relates to metaphysics and ethics, to the philosophy of history and of religion. It is, however, a necessary part of the greatness of such spiritual force that it is not like a definite scientific discovery, whose influence we can exactly measure. Rather it is so inextricably entangled with the whole culture of the time, and so closely identified with the general movement of thought, that we are increasingly unable to say what specially belongs to it alone. If we cannot estimate how much the poetical culture of modern times owes to Dante or to Shakespeare, much less can we precisely determine what, in the speculative development to which they all contribute, is respectively due to earlier philosophers, to Hegel, and to those who, since his day, have attempted to supersede, to criticise, or to complete his work. The only important question now is, not whether we are disciples of Hegel,—the days of discipleship are past,—but whether we recognise the existence of a living development of philosophy, and especially of that spiritual or idealistic view of things in which philosophy culminates—a development which begins in the earliest dawn of speculation, and in which Kant and Hegel are, not indeed the last names, but the last names in the highest order of speculative genius, *i Maestri di color che sanno.*

END OF HEGEL.